At the End of your Rope?

TIE A KNOT & HANG ON!
Help has Arrived!

CAMILLE SANZONE

For a Better Way Publishing
forabetterway@aol.com

FORWARD

My friend Camille Sanzone has written, once again, a unique and enlightened path to inner peace and wisdom with her book: <u>At the End of Your Rope? Tie a Knot and Hang On!</u> *Help has Arrived!*

Camille has made it possible to absolve the challenges we all face in our effort to be, to uncover and free the true self within. She offers ways to release our blind spots, along with the confrontations that evolve so often into self-contempt, anger and unconscious turmoil. It is then that our higher self can awaken as we transcend the dark valleys and psychological barriers through understanding and self love.

She gives us a loving, guided tour into our inner workings which ultimately frees us to balance Family, Career, Friends, Social Life, Education and Religious Life toward a re-portioning, as she so wisely expresses, to a true, forgiving and loving Authentic Self.

Camille's wisdom and insight are heightened by her spiritually enhanced poetry, her humor, and the devotion and love she has always longed to share in her lifelong quest.

As a psychotherapist and professor of Philosophy, Psychology and Comparative Religions, I am grateful and honored to be able to share Camille Sanzone's book with my patients and students!

Now open your hearts and minds, and join Camille as she guides you to your true higher self.

Valerie Pellegrini, Ph.D., LMHC

INTRODUCTION

I once heard Leo Buscaglia say, "When you think you're at the end of your rope, tie a knot and hang on!" He added: *"......and then swing!"* The hanging on is vital, of course, but the *swinging*, ah, the swinging. That one single choice adds the impulse, the notion, the idea that you are not just going to make it, you are not just going to *survive*, you are going to *thrive*, you are going to fly in the face of your seemingly insurmountable problems, and squeeze the good out of life yet!

You will find between the pages of this book a variety of life strategies, and some unabashedly uncommon wisdom, born of laughter, that will act as emotional rope for you. Take a deep breath. Help is on the way. You are going to get through this. You are going to be fine. Once you have finished reading the book, find a small piece of rope or string and keep it in your wallet. Use it as a touchstone to remind you, should you ever again feel you're at the end of your rope, that you are not, and tie a knot and hang on until the new supply arrives.

When I set out to write this book some years ago, my intention was to create strategies for living that would make life not just bearable, but delicious, or, perhaps, if you're one of those people already in a relatively good place emotionally, just *more* delicious.

You may be asking yourself right about here what makes *me* an expert in the strategies of living. I could tell you how old I am (sixty-six at this writing), that I have a great deal of life experience, that I am a non-denominational pastoral counselor, that I have been creating and facilitating workshops on personal, professional and spiritual growth, on and off, since the early eighties, but the truth is I make no claims to be an expert. I am simply a fellow traveler, making you an offer I hope you can't refuse. I am, after all, Sicilian. Do I hear strains of the theme to "The Godfather" in the background? Let's get this settled right from the start...there is no Mafia in my family. The only offer we make that you can't refuse...is for more lasagna.

What I *am* offering you here is a chance to create a life that is sacred, a life that is scrumptious, a life that is authentic and, therefore, genuinely worth living. I have learned some things in over sixty years of living that I would like to share with you, and in the words of Richard Bach, author of one of my favorite books, **Illusions: The Adventures**

of a Reluctant Messiah, *"We teach best what we most need to learn."* And so, as I share, I continue to learn too.

A popular definition of *insanity* is doing the same thing over and over again and expecting a different outcome. My goal is to make you think a little *differently* about the things that bring you pain, to focus more on the things that give you pleasure, make you laugh, sometimes because of, more often in spite of, what life brings, and, most importantly, I want to inspire you to truly *live* your life. Welcome and congratulations! Your act of picking up this book means you have chosen to search for a better way of being in the world.

[All the poetry and recipes contained in this book are my originals, unless otherwise indicated. Please check out my website: www.forabetterway.net; and listen to my weekly radio show "Tie a Knot & Hang On! HELP HAS ARRIVED!" It broadcasts live on www.w4wn.com Wednesdays at 1:00 p.m. EST. Please call in to the show or join the chat room. And I would love to hear what you think of my book. Email me at forabetterway@aol.com.]

TABLE OF CONTENTS

- APPENDIX:

  o <u>Camille's Comfort Food Recipes</u>

  o <u>One Last Process: Family Storybook</u>

  o <u>Acknowledgements</u>

  o <u>Bibliography</u>

  o <u>Suggested Reading</u>

Chapter 1

Putting one foot in front of the other

As through my mind I wander,
through haze and maze and doubt,
I dare say I do wonder
just what it's all about.
And though I'll always ponder
and pick and probe apart,
I've discovered that I'm different now;
the world is vast, but my world somehow
revolves not 'round my mind
but 'round my heart.

Ok, so what do you do when you feel like you just can't make it through one more day? You just do. You put one foot in front of the other. You take a single step. Then you take another step, and another. ***What?*** You were expecting a more complex, more grandiose dose of philosophy right off the bat? Don't worry; you can expect a few schmears of wisdom. So, I'm a Sicilian girl who knows a few Yiddish words. (I'm convinced I was Jewish in a past life, but that's a story for another book.)

Listen, some of the greatest thoughts in the universe are expressed in the simplest terms, and when it comes to getting through, keeping it simple is the way to go. As many self-help programs espouse, taking it one step at a time truly makes the most sense.

After all, when you're in the middle of severe life trauma, or are in the throes of a deep depression, perhaps are even actually contemplating suicide, there is no sense in trying to sort things out because, frankly, when you are operating in that mode, you cannot possibly see clearly enough to get yourself out of anything. There is no rhyme or reason in considering a plan of action in that frame of mind. If you had a fraction of reason left, you wouldn't be in the depths of a depression, or considering suicide. Regarding *suicide*, please know this and know it well: there is power in every moment and you can always make a new choice, unless, of course, you choose suicide. That is, if you are successful in your attempt, for then you will have, for most intents and purposes, given up all your other options. Tying the knot at the end of your rope and **hanging on**, hanging in, is, therefore, imperative.

OK, so you caught the "for **most** intents and purposes" part in the preceding paragraph, did you? The reason I inserted that is because for me to be in integrity, (see chapter 9: "LIFE: The supreme Juggling Act" re: being out of integrity and out of balance), I need to tell you that although not traditionally religious, I am spiritual. It seems more and more people are making that distinction these days. Be that as it may, I know, that is, I **sense** this in such an intense way that it has become a **knowingness** that there is more to life than this one earthly existence. No need to agree. It is safe to keep reading, so beam us back to earth, Scotty.

My good friend Mary sent me this little piece **"Does God Exist?"** - author: A. Nonymous - with her comment: **"This is the best explanation I've ever seen."**

Does God Exist?

A man went to a barbershop to have his hair cut and his beard trimmed. As the barber began to work, they began to have a good conversation. They talked about so many things and various subjects. When they eventually touched on the subject of God, the barber said: "I don't believe that God exists."

"Why do you say that?" asked the customer. "Well, you just have to go out in the street to realize that God doesn't exist. Tell me, if God exists, would there be so many sick people? Would there be abandoned children? If God existed, there would be neither suffering nor pain. I can't imagine a loving God who would allow all of these things."

The customer thought for a moment, but didn't respond because he didn't want to start an argument.

The barber finished his job and the customer left the shop. Right outside the barbershop, he saw a man in the street with long, stringy, dirty hair and an untrimmed beard. The man smelled and looked dirty and unkempt. The customer turned around and walked back into the barbershop, and he said to the barber:

"You know what? Barbers do not exist."

"That's ridiculous! How can you say that?" asked the surprised barber. "I am here, and I am a barber. And I just worked on you!"

"No!" the customer exclaimed. "Barbers don't exist because if they did, there would be no people with dirty long hair and untrimmed beards, like that man outside."

"Ah, but barbers DO exist! That's what happens when people do not come to me."

"Exactly!" affirmed the customer. "That's the point! God, too, DOES exist! That's what happens when people do not go to Him and don't look to Him for help. That's why there's so much pain and suffering in the world."

I knew where that piece was going, but couldn't help thinking of the many good, faithful people, (myself included), who do go to Him and look to Him for help, and "seemingly" - (therein lies the rub) - do not receive the answer or help they seek. There is pain and suffering in their lives. There is a bumper sticker I've seen (God's way of texting us, perhaps?) that says:

Pain is inevitable – Suffering is optional

As we go through life, we all have our troubles and pains, yet if we persist, in faith, with the hope that somehow we will make it through the difficult times, we won't suffer them as much. You may be asking: ***"But what about all those things that plague us and our families and friends? How can we not suffer through them?"*** I hear you loud and clear. Yes, for all our prayers, cancer persists and children continue to be abused, and countless other atrocities go on in this world. People, many of them good people, have addictions that appear more powerful than their will. We can find reasons not to believe every time we read a newspaper or listen to the evening news. And so, we have a choice to make. We have to choose who we want to be in the world. Do you want to be one of the ***naysayers***, the ones who see only what is wrong, who pick and probe apart everything, seeking out flaws, criticizing the parts and people they think don't fit or don't get it just right...according to them? Or would you rather be one of the ***yaysayers***, the ones who prefer to look for what's right with the world, who, while they may not wear rose-tinted glasses, still tend to see what is good about a person; one of those kind souls who are grateful for what they have, whether it is in abundance or in small measure; one of those who eagerly say *yes* to life.

In order to be one of those yaysayers, we must have faith and good expectations, and the ***hope*** that the Great Barber of life will cut our hair as needed so we can at least see our way through the "bangs" of life. (Hey, that was pretty good!)

9

While I'm at it, a few words about *hope*. I find it is highly underrated. Sometimes a new supply of rope is no more than finding *the courage to hope*. For me *hope* means:

H - Higher Consciousness
O - Overcoming
P - Pessimistic
E - Endurance

When we simply *endure* life, rather than *enjoy* it, we are, in essence, being pessimistic. We no longer look forward to happy times, to good things coming our way. When that shift takes place, no matter how slowly it may happen, and however subtle it may seem, it means we have allowed ourselves to slide into the *land of mediocrity*. That's the place we live in our heads when we only expect more of the same crap or worse. On some level of consciousness, we have come to the seemingly immutable conclusion that things will never get better, that we will never *have* enough or *be* enough. We have resigned ourselves to a life of suffering, perhaps in silence, perhaps not, but a life, nonetheless, of perpetual discontent. We become one of those people who moan, *"If I didn't have bad luck, I'd have no luck at all!"*

I would bet that at least one time in your life when you were in a very bad, even dire situation, a friend or loved one began citing reasons for you to be hopeful, only to have someone else chime in, *"Don't be giving her false hope!"*

False hope. Now that's an interesting concept. Gee, maybe I should coin a new phrase: *"If I didn't have false hope, I'd have no hope at all!"* Hope is hope. It doesn't need modifying.

Let's face it – for most of us, it is much easier to expect the worst than hope for the best. Oddly enough, allegedly wise people often give us these very odd instructions: *"Expect the worst, but hope for the best." How in the world can we, and why in the world would we, do that?* Those are two diametrically opposed thought forms. We *either* expect the worst *or* hope for the best. We cannot soberly do both simultaneously. Hoping for the best helps us to know that a new supply of rope is on the way, so that even in the face of adversity, we *can* tie a knot at the end of our rope, hang onto it, and swing on it, maybe even with a smile on our face until that new supply comes in. What we must keep in mind is that hoping, then *knowing*, that new supply is on its way is the veritable thought form necessary to create it, to manifest it into existence.

I have never been a very physical person; that is to say I have never been athletic or one to exercise regularly, unless you count *exercising caution*, which I was taught as a way of life from my very strict Sicilian father. For much of my life I was afraid to do ordinary things like roller skating, or to try new things like surfing because my mother and father had instilled in me the fear that I would get hurt. They did it out of love and concern for my wellbeing, of that I am certain, but although I, therefore, got through my childhood without a single broken bone, I was, in many ways, emotionally crippled. So, I resorted to cerebral things as a way of coping. Rather than take a walk, play softball, go swimming or roller skating with the other kids, I would read or write poetry, fool around at the piano, or do some other solitary thing. While all of those things are helpful, the quicker way to shift one's mood is to move, actually move - to take *some* sort of *action*, and, preferably something that includes other people.

Of course, when we are in the doldrums, *moving* is the last thing we want to do, and being with other people ranks second to last. We feel we *deserve* our depression or bad mood and we are darn well going to dig in our heels, which, of course, makes the rut we're already in that much deeper. Yet, over the years, I have discovered that when we make ourselves do that very thing – *move*, that is, get up, get out of bed, take a shower, go outside, take a walk, meet a friend - the chemicals in our body actually change. The levels of serotonin increase, our mood shifts, and our spirit lifts. It is what gives runners that high they speak of, and other athletes who talk about being *in the zone*. Reading doesn't do that. Writing doesn't do that. Well, actually it can for some of us. However, *laughing* certainly does it. Laughing has rightly been called *internal jogging*. Laughing *heartily*, though, not a little titter or half smile. I mean the kind of laughter Norman Cousins wrote about in **Anatomy of an Illness**. He attributed a four-hour daily regimen of watching funny videos that made him laugh out loud with helping to cure his cancer. Perhaps laughter *is* the best medicine, after all. Now if I could only learn to laugh *while* exercising. You *would* laugh if you saw *me* exercising. Trust me.

I often begin my workshops by reciting this piece from a poem written in 1513 A.D. by Brother Giovanni, an Italian monk. It was from his initiation to novitiates at the monastery, but, as you will see, it applies to all of us:

I salute you:
There is nothing I can give you which you have not got;
but there is much, very much,
that while I cannot give it, you can take.
No Heaven can come to us unless our hearts find rest in today.
Take Heaven!
No peace lies in the future which is not hidden
in this present little instant.
Take Peace!
The gloom of the world is but a shadow.
Behind it, yet within our reach, is joy,
There is radiance and glory in the darkness could we but see,
and to see, we have only to look. I beseech you to look.
And, so, at this time, I greet you. Not quite as the world sends greetings,
but with profound esteem and with prayer
that for you now and forever the day breaks,
and the shadows flee away.

(Found In **Poetry Therapy**, edited by J. Leedy, MD)

ONE-FOOT-IN-FRONT-OF-THE-OTHER PROCESS

Copy the preceding poem, leaving space for your interpretation or understanding of it after every three or four lines, as seems appropriate.

Go through the entire poem and give yourself some time. Sit with it and discover what it says *to* you and *about* you.

Example:

> ***I salute you:***
> ***There is nothing I can give you which you have not got;***
> ***but there is much, very much,***
> ***that while I cannot give it, you can take.***

What those lines mean to me is that everything I need I already have in some way.

I simply have to recognize that and take it all in.

LAUGH-OUT-LOUD EXERCISE

Mabel, a senior citizen, joined a yoga class provided at her Century Village Country Club. The instructor was so impressed with her agility; he gave her a special exercise to do between weekly classes. He instructed her to roll out her exercise mat, get completely naked, sit in the Lotus position (legs crossed beneath her), and take a few deep breaths. Then she was to gently, slowly lift her left leg and place it behind her neck, then to lift her right leg and place it behind her neck. She was to hold that position for thirty seconds.

Well, she was very excited to try this new yoga exercise, but was embarrassed to do it in front of her husband, so the very next day she waited for him to leave for his morning walk to get the newspaper.

As soon as he left, she laid down her exercise mat, took off her nightgown, and got into the Lotus position. She took several deep breaths, then very slowly, very gently, she lifted her left leg and put it behind her neck, then she did the same with her right leg.

At that very moment, the front door opened and her husband called out, "It's just me. I forgot my wallet." As he took his wallet from the hall table, he glanced in her direction and said, "Mabel, comb your hair and put your teeth in, you look just like your mother!"

So, how do we put one foot in front of the other today? One step at a time. One good laugh at a time.

LAUGHTER PROCESS

Go the library (there are still libraries, aren't there?), go on line and research jokes, or go over some I have included in the book. Find a few that are new to you and memorize them. Practice saying out loud the ones that resonate with you until you feel confident that you know them well, and then go out and tell them to people at work, to your family and friends. See the effect it has on them and on you. When I first started working as activities coordinator at a senior citizen day center in Fort Lauderdale, I initiated a "Laugh-Out-Loud" activity. At first I told some jokes and encouraged them to **laugh out loud**, even if at first it was forced, explaining to them about the power of laughter to make us feel better. Being a stand-up comedienne, I really hammed it up and sold those jokes. They loved it. Then I typed up a lot of short jokes I found on the Internet, and then cut the sheet of jokes up into strips, with one joke on each strip of paper, and I put them in a basket. I had the seniors randomly pick a piece of paper out of the basket, to read the joke they had chosen to themselves first, and then to sell it to the crowd. (They knew they could read the joke out loud if they weren't able to memorize it.) Well, they soon became hams. After I got to know their individual personalities, I sort of knew which joke fit each person, and I would assign particular jokes to each one of them. Then, going around the circle, they would each tell their joke. It was always great fun. We did that from fifteen to thirty minutes a few times a week. It became one of our favorite things to do. The seniors even started bringing in jokes, and, I have to tell you, their favorites were usually "R" rated.

Chapter 2

Why didn't *I* learn everything I needed to know in kindergarten?

My spirit is soaring;

I am so alive.

I am ruler of the world…

because today I'm five!

Life is a process, a series of pathways, a journey. A journey to a particular destination? Perhaps. I believe we were created with free will, that we have a *number* of *possible* futures. The notion that we have *a* destiny, that we are destined to do or be something in particular may be so for some of us. For some people the imprint of who they are is so clear, they know from childhood why they are here. I think the signs are there along the way for most of us, but we often have blinders on and don't recognize them for what they are. In hindsight, we may slap our spiritual foreheads, shouting, *"Aha! That's what that meant!"* I loved Robert Fulcrum's book **Everything I ever need to know I learned in Kindergarten.** It may just be that most of life's lessons can be gleaned from our first six years on this earth plane. Nonetheless, I believe we are here not so much to learn, but to rediscover what we already know to be true in the core of our beings. (Remember in my introduction I said I would be presenting some new ways of looking at life. Take it all in, keep what is worth keeping, what rings true for you, and *with the breath of kindness, blow the rest away*.) I have come to believe that the **oversoul**, or our true Self, knows everything there is to know, that we choose to incarnate in different bodies into certain life circumstances to experience all of life. Perhaps the game of life is to see how quickly we can rediscover who we really are, namely, a spiritual being in a physical body, having an earthly experience, rather than a physical being, having a spiritual experience. Once we truly know and accept who we are, we can manifest all that we desire by *knowing* what that is, and visualizing the outcome in advance. That may sound simple, but *not knowing* what we desire is perhaps the single most solid roadblock imaginable to receiving our good. You've probably heard a person or two say, *"It's not getting what I want that's so difficult; it is knowing what I want."* If we persist in sending out mixed messages, what we manifest will be a hodgepodge of events, occurrences, and things randomly pulled from the universe.

Another one of my books, which I hope to publish by the end of 2014, **EVERLASTING JOURNEY**, is a metaphysical storybook for adults. In it I describe a scene in which a couple is ordering dinner in a fine restaurant:

Server: Have you decided what you would like, Madam?

Woman: Yes, thank you. I'd like the filet mignon, with a baked potato, asparagus with Hollandaise sauce, and a glass of Cabernet Savignon.

Server: Very well, Madam; and you, Sir?

Man: I'd like the broiled salmon, the stuffed artichoke, scalloped potatoes, and a glass of White Zinfandel.

Server: Very good, Sir.

(As the server turns and is about to place their order with the chef, the woman calls to him.)

Woman: Excuse me....excuse me. Just a moment, please.

Server: Yes, Madam?

Woman: I've changed my mind. I think I'm in the mood for seafood as well. Forget the filet mignon and bring me your twin lobster tails, and that stuffed artichoke sounded lovely....with the scalloped potatoes. And make mine White Zinfandel as well.

Server: Very good, Madam.

(Again, the server starts to leave, and, this time, the man stops him.)

Man: Hold on a minute. You know, I haven't had a good piece of meat in quite a while. I think I'll have your biggest, juiciest porterhouse steak, medium rare. Keep the artichoke, but make it steak potatoes, and a glass of your house red wine.

Server: Will that be all?

Woman: Yes, thank you.

Man:	Yes, I think so.
Woman:	Well, maybe not. Dear... (she says, turning to her dinner companion) since you've decided to have steak and I originally wanted filet mignon, why don't we order the Chateau Briand for two?
Man:	Fine. Whatever you want is OK with me.
Server:	Chateau Briand for two. As you wish. Will that be steak potatoes for both of you, and two stuffed artichokes, and red wine?
Man:	Yes, that will be fine.
Woman:	No, I think with the steak I'd prefer the asparagus again, and I'll have a baked potato. The red wine is fine.

(The server leaves to place the order. This conversation ensues at the table.)

Man:	You know, maybe I ought to order surf and turf. Obviously, I wanted seafood to start with. I think I'll call our server over again and change my order.
Woman:	Well, then I'll have to change mine since you can only order Chateau Briand for two.

(The server reappears.)

Server:	Yes, how may I serve you?
Man:	We're sorry to be so much trouble, but this is our anniversary and we want this meal to be extra special. We've changed our minds again. Do you mind?
Server:	Not at all. It is my pleasure to serve you. What would you like?
Woman:	You know, the salmon he originally ordered has lingered in my mind. I think I'll have that, with asparagus and scalloped potatoes. Oh, and a glass of White Zinfandel. Yes, that will do nicely.

Man:	And I'll have the surf and turf. Lobster tails with a nice, juicy strip steak, medium rare, steak fries, your house salad with ranch dressing, and red wine.
Server:	Excellent. I'll place your orders right away.

(The server leaves and the conversation continues.)

Woman:	I know this is going to sound ridiculous, but that juicy strip steak is awfully appealing, and I haven't had lobster in ages. And this is a celebration, after all, isn't it? Do you think I dare change my order again?
Man:	We're paying the bill. We should get what we want.

(Once again, the server is summoned and reappears.)

Man:	We've changed our minds again. The lady would like the surf and turf as well. But make her steak well done.
Woman:	And to make it easy for you, I'll have the house salad with ranch dressing, steak fries and red wine. Thank you.
Server:	As you wish.
Man:	You know, I think I've changed my mind again too. I'll just have the porterhouse steak, after all. I'm not really in the mood for lobster tails.
Server:	Very good, sir. Will that be all?
Woman:	Well..........

And so on and so on. They continue to change their order until the restaurant is about to close and they are asked to leave. They storm out of the restaurant complaining bitterly that they haven't yet been served, go home hungry, angry and disappointed, and wind up dining on leftovers from their refrigerator.

Now, consider the universe, God, whatever or wherever you send your prayers, your wishes and dreams, place your orders, focus your attention—as the Server in the foregoing dialog. The Server is unbiased. The Server is there to *serve* you. The Server will change your order as many times as you wish, but the Server cannot bring you anything particular if your order is not clear, if you are not sure what it is you want. When we don't know what we want, we live life in the *land of mediocrity*, getting the hodgepodge the universe randomly selects instead of the life we could design for ourselves. What we are talking about here is clear intention, focused attention, followed by relevant action in the direction of our dream or desire.

Haven't you seen someone succeed who is less talented or less able than you? Haven't you wondered, *"How in the world did she manage that?"* Persistence of thought and action in combination is very powerful. If our talent and skill remain unfocused, persistence, or perseverance, can be a stronger magnet than even extraordinary amounts of talent and skill. We instinctively know that intention and perseverance are indomitable allies, yet many of us fail to live up to our potential. If necessity is, indeed, the mother of invention, then, perhaps, *creativity is the child of intention*. Yes, yes, I know, we have all heard the expression, *"The road to hell is paved with good intentions."* To reinforce the idea, I am talking here about *clear* intention, followed by real and persistent action, with a focused attention on what we want to draw into the circle of our lives.

In **EVERLASTING JOURNEY**, I also talk about a suitcase that we all carry throughout life. One of the items among the contents of our life suitcase is *a bag of potentials*. Printed on the back of the bag is this warning: *You may not reach all your potential in one lifetime, but unless you reach in and stretch on a regular basis, this bag will shrivel up.* Another item is a box of chocolate-covered *I Can'ts*. Now that alone is incentive to go on a mental diet. No more *I Can'ts*, please! One of the most effective ways to alter our behavior is to replace *can't* with *won't*. Rather than surrendering and bemoaning our limitations by saying over and over again *I can't, I simply can't do that*, claim the power that comes when we acknowledge that our behavior is within our control, that it is our *choice* not to do or not do something. It's simple really, but the error in our thinking is that simple means *easy*. Simple *ain't* always easy - at least not at first. Another item in the suitcase is a recording of a country western tune I wrote called, *"Don't let the world SHOULD on you!"* The refrain goes, *"No matter what they say you ought to, and no matter what they do....stand up for who you are and don't let the world SHOULD on you!"*

THINGS-I'VE-LEARNED-TO-BE-TRUE PROCESSES

1. Imagine you are a time traveler and are about to go visit your six-year-old self. Write down what you would say to yourself. Perhaps you would tell yourself how good you are, how bright, how creative, how loved you are. Say only positive things, things that might better prepare you for a sweeter, more fulfilling life.

    Now imagine your adult self holding your six-year-old self in your lap as you tell them from the depths of your heart what you would have wanted to hear.

2. Take two sheets of paper. At the top of each write THINGS I'VE LEARNED TO BE TRUE. Underneath one write NEGATIVE, and on the other, write POSITIVE.

    Example:

    THINGS I'VE LEARNED TO BE TRUE
    (Negative)
    We can't always be happy.
    We can't have everything.
    We were born to suffer.

    THINGS I'VE LEARNED TO BE TRUE
    (Positive)
    Things are never as bad as they seem.
    I am much loved.
    I am talented.
    Life is good.
    Life is sacred and has meaning.

Write until you at least fill the page, but write as much as you want. Flip the page over and keep writing if you feel so inspired. When you finish, take a good look at both lists. Which list is longer? Which list steers you? What have you learned to be true that most consistently determines your experience of life? Write a paragraph or two about it.

Chapter 3

Living on the Verge: Change without Crisis

Rock-a-bye, baby…
could this be all?
Ah, bedded tranquility...
Be careful, don't fall!
Vanishing virgin,
taken into hell...
violated, broken...
I hungered. and I fell.
Rock-a-bye, baby...
when does it stop?
White mountains of air...
from bottom to top.
Up from the dredges,
crucifying, mortifying.
Rising higher. sinking in dismay.
Out with imaginings…
idealistic, flowerific...
wake up and see the world
before it goes away.

What a concept! What a novel idea: Change *without* Crisis.

What is it about change that rattles us so? Change is often the spice of life, the stuff that gets our juices flowing. Change can be seen as an adventure; it can be the beginning of a new chapter in our lives. Aha…*new?* (For my Jewish readers, *nu?*)

Therein lies the rub! *New often means unknown*, untried...and we are usually unwilling to undo or unsettle the familiar framework within which we operate, in which we live, even if it seems exciting. Oddly enough, even if the way we are living is not pleasing to us, we often decide to keep things status quo because change breeds stress, sometimes good stress, sometimes bad stress, but stress, nonetheless. For some of us *"Familiarity breeds contempt,"* but for many more it breeds *content* or, more accurately, it breeds *complacency*. How many times in our lives have we heard: ***"Don't rock the boat."*** ***"Don't make waves." "Don't upset the applecart." "Don't get beyond your station in life." "Don't you ever stop wanting more?"*** We would serve ourselves well by rephrasing all of those and putting a new tape into our programming: ***"Don't hesitate." "Make waves. "Rock the darn boat! Upset the applecart!" "Go beyond...and don't ever stop wanting more!"*** (For a good, fun read, get Bette Midler's fantastically illustrated book, **The Saga of Baby Divine**…it's about a baby who wants *more*.)

Living ***on the verge*** is hardly living on the Riviera. Although I confess to visiting the verge a few times, it's one of those places you're not sure you've been until you're on your way back from it. I assure you it is neither a nice place to visit or live. Too much tension—good and bad.

We've all heard the expression, ***"I'm on the verge of something great happening."*** We've also heard: ***"I'm on the verge of a nervous breakdown."*** In the first statement, being ***on the verge*** appears to be a positive place to be, full of excitement and anticipation, albeit usually far off in the distance, even though we sense we're ***on the verge*** of it happening. In the second statement, being ***on the verge*** is frighteningly imminent, like being about to fall from the edge of a cliff.

I went to the New World Dictionary of the American Language for a definition. In part, this is what I found:

Verge: the edge, brink, a bend, twist, margin (as the verge of the forest), an enclosing line or border, a boundary of something more or less circular.

When we're always ***on the verge***, we never arrive; we feel like an almost ran, a has-been who never was. It's going through life with a thousand things on your mind, and none of them coming to fruition. It's that right answer, the eloquent phrase that lingers on the tip of your tongue, then dissolves like a bitter pill, absorbed into your system, unuttered and usually irretrievable.

Being ***on the verge*** can make us dizzy as 'round and 'round we go because it means we're dwelling in the land of possibilities. Possibilities can, of course, be wonderful, and being ***on the verge*** of something can be exhilarating, but we must finally shift into the next gear and go from being ***on the verge*** of greatness to the place where our *mojo* is working. That is, of course, unless the verge we're on is the one leading to a nervous breakdown. And even then, if we listen to the sage advice of playwright Jane Wagner's bag lady, as portrayed by Lily Tomlin in ***"The Search for Signs of Intelligent Life in the Universe,"*** a nervous break*down*, if viewed from the proper angle, can be a break*through*.

So, whether we feel we are at the end of our rope or on the verge of some real or imagined pending doom, how do we hang on, how do we get beyond that verge, go around the bend, cross that border, and obliterate that boundary completely? Are we required to take that empty-handed, but full-hearted leap of faith into the void? Perhaps, sometimes; but just maybe *the answer lies in simply changing our perspective*. Changing the way we think about time, for instance, can often make all the difference.

Are you hypercritical about how you use your time? Does everything you do have to be task oriented? If you spend time doing something creative, something not on your to-do list, do you feel you wasted, rather than spent that time well? Do you live your life doing only those things that spell obligation or fall under the umbrella of "have to" and wind up feeling like you're "doing time," a veritable prisoner in a cage of your own making?

Do you teeter on the edge of time, living *on the verge*, nervously, anxiously waiting for that right moment to happen, the one that transforms your life for the better forever?

I suspect more of us live our lives that way rather than having the peace of mind of knowing that we are doing the best we can, and that as long as we are on planet earth, we are *works in progress*.   As for me, I waver from knowing I'm a work in progress to feeling that *I'm just a piece of work*. In any case, I sense *"The kingdom of heaven is at hand."*

It has a lot to do with learning to enjoy the present moment, without regrets about past experience or worries about what might yet go wrong. Maybe it's as simple as "Surrendering the How," (as I suggest in Chapter 8), and trusting that all will unfold as it should. Uh oh. There's that naughty word SHOULD again.

Freedom is looking at the past
with neither regret nor longing somehow,
content to live in the power of now.

In the *mean*time, (A curious phrase that. I guess time does sometimes seem *mean* when we are waiting impatiently, doesn't it?), along with all the other things we do with our days, we can choose to bring into our world more of the activities we enjoy, more of what we love to do. Then we will be spiritual millionaires of time, for each moment will be precious. We will not tremble on the verge. OK…we may for a moment, but then we will soar above it and beyond it.

CHANGE-WITHOUT-CRISIS PROCESS

Leaving space between each, write down five big changes that have taken place in your life: a move, a new job, a marriage, a divorce, a pregnancy, or, perhaps, an illness.

After each one, describe your emotions around that change. For example: Did you go to a new job because you were fired, because you were so stressed out you became sick and had to quit, or because you found another, better job which suited your talents and worth?

Whatever instigated the change, how did you feel about it? How did you react to it?

From your responses to the five big changes you list, write an essay answering this question: How do you generally make changes or handle changes in your life? Do you dread them or welcome them?

Chapter 4

Get Off Your "BUT"

Poetry in motion…
is such a nice notion,
but how do I get myself to move?
I may say, "I've got nothing to prove,"
but I've got to get into the groove.
Goethe said, "Whatever you can do…..begin it..."
and while I believe that in my gut,
there are times inertia enslaves me.
and I just can't get off my BUT.

"Whatever you can do, or dream you can, begin it.
Boldness has genius, power, and magic in it. "
Johann Wolfgang von Goethe

You know that infamous "BUT," don't you? I would like to change jobs, *but* I'm afraid to try something new. I'd love to go to college, *but* I don't think I could get passing grades. I'd love to go out with that person, *but* what would they ever see in me?

So how do we get off our BUT?
(a) by doing what is hard for us to do
(b) by following our bliss
(c) by serving humanity doing that which we love to do and do well
(d) by sharing with the world the gifts and talents with which we have been bestowed

or (e) all of the above

I hope you answered ***all of the above***, for it is the correct answer. Sometimes we get off our ***but*** simply by getting off our butt and taking action in the direction of our dreams.

When do we get in the most trouble?

(a) when we adhere to only one way of doing things

(b) when our philosophical horse wears blinders so it won't be frightened or distracted by anything else

(c) when we delude ourselves into believing we know something nobody else does?

(d) when we pretend to be in control, when what better serves us is to surrender to what feels right?

or (e) all of the above

Did you say *all of the above*? You're catching on! Still, I can hear you saying, ***"Oh, but just because a thing feels right, does not make it so."*** God forbid, (pun intended), we should do what feels right! Now I'm not talking about what the religious RIGHT (wrong!) says is right, I'm referring to ***what feels right for us personally***. There are those who might call that ***moral particularism***, or situational morality, but I have more faith in the goodness of humanity to think that if we had no laws and no commandments, the world would be a place of mayhem. Of course, the kind of world to which I allude, and, perhaps, for which I long, requires that children be raised with the notion that doing right for its own sake is its own reward, not just because you won't be thrown in jail, go to hell or otherwise be punished if you don't "do right."

We would do well to teach children that ***character*** is more important than ***reputation***, for character is who we ***are;*** reputation is who others ***think*** we are.

Far too often we ignore our gut feeling, the hunch, the instinct that tells us to follow that path, make this choice. We so seldom listen to that still small voice speaking to us inside our heads that the voice becomes an inaudible whisper, until the hunches cease to come. We do that because somewhere along the line our ***bullshit detector*** was turned off. When we are little, we can smell it right away, but somewhere along the way we accepted the reality with which we were presented and started to believe that we could not trust ourselves. We started to think thoughts like*: **"I feel in my gut that this is what I want to do, BUT what will people think, how will I support myself, who do I think I am?"***

There are no easy answers if we've been bitten by the ***but***, (or ***on the butt)***, for most of our lives, but if ***you*** are waiting for a big, booming, resounding voice to come from the Heavens telling you what it is you need to do, you will likely have a long wait. However, if you choose to look at life and yourself differently, if you change your mind about how things ***can*** be, the world you see ***will*** change before your eyes.

We were given free will to live this life with parameters that are unlimited. (Oops, that sounds like an oxymoron....unlimited parameters.) How sad that something as delicious as freedom can turn sour for so many of us. Some of us are so frightened to death of making wrong choices, that we make no choices and eventually stagnate in our own spiritual paralysis.

If you truly did not want to get beyond the inertia which is your life as it is, you would not have chosen to read this book. You **can** do the work you need to do to jumpstart your life, and you can **choose** to do it with so much love in your heart for your inner child that it becomes play for both of you.

I recommend Julia Cameron's book **THE ARTIST'S WAY**. At the end of each chapter, she suggests an exercise for you to try. One of those things is taking yourself on a date once a week. You read that correctly: take yourself on a date, do something **by** yourself that you would enjoy doing. It can be anything: going for a walk in the park, taking in a movie, going to a museum, trying that new bistro, sitting on a blanket at the beach, or in the woods.

If you want good relationships with others, you must first forge one with yourself. Learn to enjoy your own company. Go on! You have nothing to lose but your despair.

GET-OFF-YOUR-BUT PROCESS

Make a conscious decision to get off your BUT. Stop saying, *"That might work for some people, **BUT**......it's not for me."* or *"That sounds OK when **you** say it, **BUT** things just never work out for **me**."*

Create a list of twenty things you ever even remotely considered might be fun or interesting to do. Commit to trying one of them every week or, at least, once a month. Give it all you've got.

Most importantly, don't give up on yourself before you even start by telling yourself nothing interests you. Life is not boring except to those who **are** boring. And you are boring only if you refuse to savor life, to drink from its fountain. There's a line I love in the movie **"Auntie Mame."** Rosalind Russell, as Mame, tells her dowdy secretary Agnes Gooch (played by Peggy Cass) to **"Live! Life is a banquet and most poor suckers are starving to death!"**

Don't starve yourself! Discover what you find delicious in this life. Learn what tickles you, what makes you laugh. Rent and watch different movies. Observe your reactions. Look in the newspaper in the local events section. Perhaps a group that meets weekly will strike a chord with you. **Participate** in your life in a **proactive** way. Nobody is going to be your perpetual social director, it is up to **you**!

Go on, put the book or tablet down, or get out of your computer task chair. Get off your butt, and, more importantly, get off your **BUT!** Go write that list and then **do** something, something fun, something interesting, perhaps, even something **different**.

Chapter 5

There is POWER in every Moment

If we only knew the power
of the simple words I am,
we would become all the wonderful things
we earnestly believe we can.

For the things we say most often
once the words I am are spoken,
set in motion a mystical force...
one not easily broken.

So, when you hear yourself begin to say
the words I am, beware!
Say only things you want to be...
Learn to choose your words with care.

Sometimes power comes from the simple choice to say "YES" to life. YES! YES! YES! Perhaps those three yeses conjure up the scene in the diner from the movie, "When Harry Met Sally," where Meg Ryan's character is simulating the sounds of an orgasm to Billy Crystal's character to prove that women can and do fake orgasms. The analogy holds true to all of life. When we are not committed, when we choose to *fake it*, we truly only cheat ourselves.

The word YES has transformative powers. When said from joy and a genuinely open reception to life's possibilities, it can and does move us in wonderful directions. These days we seem more apt to hear about learning to say NO. We pay attention to what we should **not** do, when we would be better served if we would focus on the positive, life affirming experiences offered to us. We often stumble upon potentially exhilarating new ventures, but, sadly, more often than not, our gloomy toxic self almost immediately comes up with ten reasons why we should not follow our instinct to go for it.

Of course, there is a stark contrast in saying YES to life and NO to things that would deplete us or harm us. The trick is in knowing when a YES is truly a YES, when a YES is really a NO, when a NO is truly a NO, and when a NO is a yearning to say YES. Have I made that dreadfully unclear?

Fear and love too commonly dwell within most of us. When we come from fear, we tend to settle for a life that doesn't fit us, and we wind up surviving instead of thriving, existing instead of blissing. For some people being a SURVIOR becomes their whole persona, and while I understand and respect the strength there is, for a time, in identifying as a SURVIVOR…of child sexual abuse, spousal abuse, cancer, on and on, I think there comes a time when we need to take off the mantle of SURVIVORHOOD and get on with life. We cannot perpetually identify as a VICTIM without at least remotely expecting life to disappoint us or hurt us yet again.

Then there are others who, while they don't identify as SURVIVORS or VICTIMS, live a life they think they are **supposed** to live. Society's child, the good daughter, obedient son, thoughtful husband, the responsible father, dutiful wife, the sacrificing mother, whatever the label inside the invisible cloak we wear, we routinely answer YES when we want to say NO, and say NO when we would love to say YES.

I have known people who chose to stay in unhappy marriages rather than confront their partner for fear they would open wounds that would never heal. They would not let themselves express their true feelings, telling themselves they loved their partner, even if they were no longer in love with them and chose to remain married primarily because neither of them would be able to have the home, lifestyle, and creature comforts living on their individual incomes that they enjoyed with their combined incomes. I get that, but is it worth it to live a life in quiet desperation, discontented and depressed? That trifecta - Discontent - Desperation – Depression - is a 3-D version of life I would avoid at all costs - even being alone and living more modestly. I think if there is a foundation of genuine love, an honest and raw heart-to-heart talk might prove pivotal in engendering real growth and change.

I am not suggesting that wives leave their husbands, or husbands shirk their responsibilities and abandon their families. What I am suggesting is that too many people fall into a rut that just gets deeper with time, so deep they cannot see a way out, and suddenly one day feel as though they've come to the end of their rope.

When we do only what is expected of us, or what we *think* is expected of us, we make choices that squeeze the life out of us because they neither nourish nor sustain us. The tragedy is that *we soon forget what it was that we were passionate about in the first place, what it was that filled us with joy, who it was we intended to be.* We fall asleep at the wheel of life, become depressed or, worse, we become emotionally paralyzed, walk through our lives, but not really live it. We may secretly look to fortune cookies, psychics and lotteries to guide and save us, but life is not meant to be a walkthrough. *Life is to be lived with gusto!*

Wouldn't it be delicious to create a life where we actually say YES when we mean it and NO when it serves us? I hear some of you thinking: *"But it is selfish to say NO when people ask us to do things for them."* No, it is not, not if we say NO appropriately. Oh, I suppose we'll never completely lose our sense of obligation to particular people in certain circumstances, and, perhaps, that is as it *ought* to be. (Notice I avoided using the word "should" – as you know, I don't like it when life *shoulds* on us!) And so, of course, we all say YES on some occasions even when we'd prefer to say NO, and that may just be a *part* of life, but surely not the whole of it.

Isn't it time to rely on your internal barometer which tells you if you are saying YES out of a genuine *desire to compromise*, or, if you are *being compromised* by saying YES?

BIG DIFFERENCE. HUGE DIFFERENCE.

Compromising is fair and can produce win-win situations; *being compromised* is doing something that we know is wrong or wrong for us, something that tarnishes our integrity, or diminishes us in some important way. When we allow ourselves to be compromised too often, we are essentially *putting ourselves in our pockets* where breathing itself becomes so labored that we forget or lose who we are. Ironically, we then become resentful of those very people we sought to please. We now blame them for whatever it is we think we have missed out on in our lives. (For more on "compromising without being compromised," see the section on <u>Nourishing the Soul</u> in Chapter 16.)

Why not vow to say YES more to those life-affirming urges that have stayed dormant too long in the corners of your soul? You can heal your wounded spirit by loving yourself enough to say YES and to say NO when either word truly needs uttering.

If there are too many worn out crayons in your box, get new ones and dare to draw outside of the lines. If some crayons have never been used, dare to paint a new canvas for your life. If you feel trapped, broken, lost or in hiding, take a deep breath of life and say YES! YES! YES!

Perhaps you've heard about the man who went to a psychiatrist because he believed he was suffering from an inferiority complex. After a thorough consultation, the psychiatrist told the man he had good news and bad news for him. Eager to hear the good news, the man sat up straight in his chair.

"OK, Doc, what's the good news?"

"The good news is you do **not** have an inferiority complex."

"I don't? Well, that's wonderful! So, what's the **bad** news?"

"The bad news is you really **are** inferior."

Now let's flip that and look at it another way. Imagine yourself going to see a spiritual counselor, similarly concerned, but instead of an inferiority complex, you are troubled by thinking you have a **messiah complex**. The counselor tells you, **"I have good news and great news for you. The good news is you do not have a messiah complex. The great news is you truly are a messiah."**

The operative word in that last sentence is "a" – the spiritual counselor did not say "the" messiah, but "a" messiah, for I believe we are, in essence, all co-creators of our own lives. By the thoughts we think most often, and the way we react to the circumstances around us, we create the life we live.

A spiritual truism I love is that we don't get what we deserve, we get what we most consistently **believe** we deserve.

Mark Twain said, **"Faith is believing what we know can't possibly happen."** Remember that you can always choose again. You can choose to believe something else. You can choose to believe that something good will happen, and then act according to that new belief.

Living in the present moment is essential to a full and happy life, but a basic component of happiness is having good things to look forward to. Having the expectation of more good times enhances the present moment.

We've all heard the expressions *"hoping against hope," and "hoping for the best, but expecting the worst."* Some people even warn us not to give people *false* hope. Well, I believe *hope* may just be the mother of *belief. **Believing*** a thing is so or will come to pass, or, better still, has already happened on some strata of universal existence, *is key* to bringing that thing from a thought (desire, wish) into reality. Even in the bible, we are told to *pray believing* the thing we pray for is already ours. That kind of praying goes beyond believing, beyond faith. That is taking the proverbial, often empty-handed, leap of faith into the void at the precise point where faith is converted into a certainty which surpasses all hope, faith and understanding. That was the moment we saw depicted so brilliantly in the movie "Raiders of the Lost Ark" when Harrison Ford's character, Indiana Jones, takes that literal leap across the void. At that moment, in one flash of an instant, faith evaporated into certainty and the thing was accomplished.

We've all experienced those rare and wonderful moments of being in spiritual sync with the universe, haven't we? Those moments when we sense we're running on all cylinders, when we instinctively know what to do, when to do it, where to do it, with whom to do it, or to whom to do it. *Yeah, Baby!* You get the picture. Why can't we live in such a way that those moments come more regularly? Why can't we live life more consciously in a way that strings together those blessed, sacred moments into a magnificent pearl necklace of a life? Point of fact is *we can*!

The world can literally be our oyster, but we have to seek out the pearls in order to string them together; otherwise, we live randomly, finding a pearl here and there, a fragment of bliss every once in a long, long while. We have to *live proactively*, and not just with faith, but with a *certainty* that the universe, (God, or whatever higher power resonates with you), is *for* us. Albert Einstein believed that the way we answer this one question determines the experience of life we create for ourselves: *"Is the Universe friendly?"* In other words: *Do you believe the universe is for you or against you?*

I believe Einstein was right to pose that question, for our response to that one question frames the way we view the world and our place in it. Our answer to that one question has the power to empower us or cripple us.

One way of taking back your power then is to say YES to life. Another is to know that you *can always choose again.* The power to make a change in your life is in every moment.

POWER PROCESS

Take a moment and decide what it is you want to change about your life. Start small if you like. Perhaps you've become bored with the route you take to work. Explore other options for a week. Perhaps you feel it's time to mend fences with someone. Write a letter or make a phone call asking for forgiveness or giving it. Challenge yourself to speak the truth for an entire day, and then stretch that to a week, a month. Read or re-read **The Four Agreements: A Practical Guide to Personal Freedom,** by Don Miguel Ruiz. Write an essay describing how it applies to your life.

Make this moment your moment of power.

AN AHA MOMENT

An out-of-towner accidentally drove his car into a deep ditch on the side of a country road. Luckily a farmer happened by with his big old horse named Benny.

The man asked for help. The farmer said Benny could pull his car out. So he backed Benny up and hitched Benny to the man's car bumper.

Then he yelled, "Pull, Nellie, pull." Benny didn't move. Then he yelled, "Come on, pull Ranger." Still, Benny didn't move. Then he yelled really loud, "Now pull, Fred, pull hard." Benny just stood there.

Then the farmer nonchalantly said, "Okay, Benny, pull."

Benny pulled the car out of the ditch.

The man was very appreciative but curious. He asked the farmer why he called his horse by the wrong name three times.

The farmer said, "Oh, Benny is blind, and if he thought he was the only one pulling, he wouldn't even try."

Chapter 6

Believe it or Not

Why do mortals laugh when on the inside they cry?
Why don't they learn to live, when all too soon they die?
Why can't they show affection, why won't they lend a hand?
It's a tragic imperfection, not easy to understand.
Why can't they hand out praise when a fellow human rises?
Instead they often stand in line to be the first who criticizes.
Why don't they take the time to care about life's wondrous things,
like sunsets and daffodils, a bird that sweetly sings?
It really is amusing in a sad and somber way
how generation follows generation when they don't know enough to enjoy each day.

Norman Vincent Peale once wrote, "Whether you think you can or you think you can't, you're right." Just substitute the word "believe" for "think." What do *you* believe to be true about yourself, about life? It's been written that what we fear most will come upon us. Well, you can substitute "believe" for "fear" too. Choose whichever word works for you. When we are told to pray unceasingly for that which we want to bring into our lives, what is truly meant is that we are to summon up in us a vision of what we desire with clear intent, and we are to do that consistently. I used to think "unceasingly" meant "constantly," and that seemed obsessive to me. Now I understand that it means consistently, regularly, often. When we choose to entertain our minds and souls with thoughts and visions of what we truly want, it *will*, it *must* manifest for us. Does that sound trite or trivial? You would not be reading this book if that were the case for you. What fills your soul? What thoughts linger in your mind? What is it you say most frequently to yourself? Oh, you don't talk to yourself? Not *you*. Of course not. Well, of course you do! We all do, all the time! Don't believe me? OK. Stop reading for a few minutes. Just sit quietly with your thoughts and listen. STOP READING ALREADY!

Did you try it? Well, that little voice inside your head saying over and over again, *"I don't hear anything. There's no small voice inside MY head."* That is *you* talking to yourself. There is a running conversation going on all the time. We are constantly monitoring, editing, criticizing, judging, loving, approving, disapproving, and congratulating ourselves for everything we do or say or think of doing. So, why not make it time well spent? There is a wonderful little booklet by Emmet Fox called *"The 7-day Mental Diet."* (While I'm at it, let me also recommend another of his pamphlets *"Your Heart's Desire."*) In his *"7-day Mental Diet,"* he asks us to choose only positive thoughts for 7 days, and guarantees us that if we are successful in doing that, it will forever change our lives for the better. He says if we find ourselves thinking a negative thought, we are to start all over again. I don't think it's necessary to be that hard on ourselves. I think if we have made the conscious decision to try the mental diet, we should accept the fact that we may, from time to time, sense a negative thought floating by.

What makes the difference is what we do when that happens.

a) Do we allow ourselves to entertain that thought?
b) Do we obsessively dwell on it?
c) Do we acknowledge its presence, even thank it for stopping by, and then choose to dismiss it?

A way I've found to do that is to simply say to myself, *"Cancel...cancel!"* And then I go on to something else. The point is to become aware of the trends in our thinking, to become our own life coach. Rather than knocking ourselves or putting ourselves down, let's begin again to love ourselves, to encourage ourselves.

Look at some of the stuff participants in a workshop I did years ago had to say about the things they heard themselves saying to themselves all day long:

- I'm such an idiot!
- Who am I kidding...I can't do this!
- I am going to mess this up, I just know it.
- I am not going to pass this test.
- I'll probably louse up this relationship too.
- I am such a loser!
- My head is killing me.

Is it any wonder we sometimes pull so much crap into our lives?

Perhaps you've heard the expression, "Hitch your wagon to a star!" Ralph Waldo Emerson described it beautifully this way:

Now that is the wisdom of a man, in every instance of his labor, to hitch his wagon to a star, and see his chore done by the gods themselves. That is the way we are strong, by borrowing the might of the elements. The forces of steam, gravity, galvanism, light, magnets, wind, fire, serve us day by day and cost us nothing.

In other words, we are made stronger by the notion or belief that God, the universe, the very elements of nature, are assisting us in our every action; they are veritably conspiring on our behalf. Emerson's star *will* carry us, it will take us where we need and want to go.

We are never truly alone, and, therefore, never really at the end of our rope…and for that very same reason. To grasp that fully, however, it is essential that we take the time to explore what the other end of our rope is fastened to, to know what star guides us, what root belief truly anchors us. What are you bound by? What do you know to be true, what are your core values, those which determine how you represent yourself in the world? What limits have you placed on yourself, wittingly or, more likely, unwittingly?

We may be fastened to our family by such a steadfast love and commitment that we lose sight of everything else in our lives which we also value. Loving with that kind of intensity can be powerful and wonderful…for a time, but it can also create disaster if something goes wrong with our relationship, or something terrible happens to someone in our family. If that one relationship or our family is the only thing to which we are significantly fastened, we may literally become unhinged. The rope swings free and we feel we are hanging by a thread. Some people would say the only thing that serves us, the only thing which can sustain us throughout our lives is our faith in a higher power, for all intents and purposes, God. But doesn't even our faith in God waver? Sure it does. And, let's not forget that some of us don't believe in God at all. What's an agnostic or atheist to believe in at those times?

Chapter 7

AFFIRMATIONS: Telling the Truth in Advance

Wishing and hoping for something more…
what a futile preoccupation.
The SECRET, as many are now discovering,
is knowing the thing is yours.
Envision as already present
that which you most desire!
Imagination's fire
burns inside you all the time.
All you have to do to
fan the flames higher
is
affirm it,
activate the power!
Claim it!
And life's gifts upon you
will be showered!

Does the Universe play favorites? Just as gravity is no respecter of persons, the universe does not play favorites either; at least, not exactly. You've heard the expression, *"Everybody loves a winner."* Well, so does the universe. Not that the universe plays favorites, but the *winner* personality has the *consciousness* of a winner, the *attitude* of a winner, the *mindset* of a winner, and, therefore, the *outcome* of a winner, at least, more often than not.

I was a lay catechist in a Catholic church in my early twenties and I taught religious instruction to a class of eleven year olds every Saturday morning for an entire school year. One day one of the boys in my class very astutely posed this question: *"If two baseball teams both pray to God to win before a baseball game, how does God choose which team will win?"* I took a moment to think about his question and while I thought about it, I asked the class to think about it, too, and to write down the answer that came to them.

Most of the children came up with theories ranging from....God said yes to the team with the highest number of Catholics on it, to whichever team had practiced harder. My theory was and still is that God would not choose one of His children over another. The concept of God with which I resonate is one that allows each of us to receive according to our belief, and so the team with the most members who prayed *knowing they would receive the outcome they were praying for* is the team that would win.

Those who pray beating their chest....asking in one breath for the cherished thing they desire and in the next breath announce they are unworthy to receive it...are doomed to a lifetime of *seemingly* unanswered prayer. It is not really unanswered at all. Sometimes God answers prayers with No. More accurately, Universal Law, the Law of Attraction, or, as some people now refer to it "The Secret," is set up so that we get what we pray for when our thinking is consistently right. It is not a trick or a game; it is just the Law at work.

If you read a book about or hear a lecturer speak about positive thinking, you are asked to become aware of your self talk or back talk. That's the little voice inside your head I told you about earlier. Well that voice also responds when you say an affirmation. For example, I might say, *"I am happy. I am healthy. I am wealthy. I am wise."* And the little voice in my head might respond, *"Yeah, sure, you sad, fat, poor stupid bastard!"* So how effective would that affirmation be? Even if I were to say it a thousand times...as long as that little voice kept following it with *"Yeah, sure...."* – what would be the point? It would be an effort in futility.

A lot of people get bogged down with affirmations because they feel uncomfortable saying things they know to be untrue. The way around that is to know ***you are telling the truth in advance***. That is, after all, what an affirmation essentially is. It is a statement of that which you want to bring into your life, the truth about who you are in the core of your being. It is praying for something, knowing that it is already yours; in other words, it is telling what you truly believe to be the truth, but in advance.

My father died at home, which is what he wanted. Hospice had delivered a hospital bed and they were giving him "comfort care." Finally, he was not responding at all, and we were all gathered around him. He seemed to be hanging on for us, so I took Mom out of the room and asked her to tell Dad that we had won the lottery. Dad used to play religiously. My mother objected at first, saying, "But that's a lie. You want me to lie to your father?" I said, "Mom, we may very well win some day. Think of it as telling the truth in advance. Knowing we will all be taken care of will give Dad some peace. I think he'll be able to let go."

We went back into the room. Mom leaned over the hospital bed and, in a stage whisper so loud we could all hear, said, "Hon, we won the lottery. SEVENTEEN MILLION DOLLARS!"

I had to laugh. She didn't want to lie, but if she was going to tell the truth in advance, I guess she figured it might as well be a big one. I don't play the lottery with the same intensity Dad did, but you can be sure I play when the amount is $17,000,000. The numbers I play to create the six numbers are a combination of Dad's birth date and mine.

Dad played the lottery very seriously. He had a book in which he wrote down the series of numbers he played every week, but did he truly believe he would ever win? I don't think so.

Do you think we get what we deserve? Did my father deserve to win the lottery? Of course I think so. We don't get what we deserve in this life; we get what we think we deserve in the deepest recesses of our being.

Aren't there times when you just can't understand why someone you perceive as less deserving than you seems to be getting so much more of the good in life? Well, that is the LAW at work. Once again: FLASH BULLETIN...we don't get what we deserve....we get what we *think, believe, know for a certainty in our gut,* we deserve. Yes, it always comes back to our thoughts being creative, but in addition to our thoughts, the back talk in our head must be in sync, or in alignment. Our whole being must resonate with that thought. I'm not a literalist and I certainly am not a Bible thumper, recovering Catholic that I am, but even in the Bible it says to "pray without ceasing." I don't believe that is what that expression means. It does not mean that we must consciously "pray" in some ritualistic way every moment of the day, but that we keep as an ever-present thought form, in our innermost being, the thing we desire to have or to be.

Of course, we can't expect our good to come to us if we don't know consistently what that good is. When we are really stymied and can't quite figure out what it is we want most, it is probably best to ask or pray for the thing we think fits the bill, but then tack on to our prayer or affirmation....*this or something better that is for my highest good and the highest good of all concerned.*

Remember: affirmations are "Telling the truth in advance." This is not creative accounting. This is not fabricating outlandish tales about who we are. This is not telling ourselves untruths or conning ourselves. This is affirming that which we want, or that which we want to be, and stating it as if it already is. Affirming what we want to manifest in our lives by stating it in the present tense; i.e., "I *am* happy," rather than "I am *going to be happy when*...." is a powerful tool in creating, or manifesting the thing we want or want to be. It has to do with belief for sure, but the ingredient most of us miss all too often is focus. It is absolutely vital to have a clear, consistent intention and passion

40

about it, a feeling deep it in our gut! If we believe that there are laws in the universe that respond to our thoughts, then we must believe, too, that it takes things literally. Therefore, if I consistently think or pray, "I want to have..." or "I want to be..." or if we take a trip to Someday Isle....and say, *"Someday I'll* have money..." or *"Someday I'll* find true love" ...what we do is perpetuate the state or condition of *wanting* the thing, not having it.

When we do that, all we do is keep pushing our wants into the future, keeping that which we want at arms length; for, in fact, when we *want* something, it indicates that we currently *lack* it. I know what you're thinking: "Why is it so tricky, so complicated? Is the universe, God with all Her little Gods, Goddesses and Fairies just playing semantics with us?" You would think God knows our innermost thoughts and that when we say we want something, we don't mean we lack it, we mean we *wan*t it, and usually RIGHT NOW. I suppose you have heard the prayer of the impatient man: "God, give me patience. And give it to me RIGHT NOW!"

Well, God...the Universe…your Higher Self, whatever power to which you subscribe, does know your innermost thoughts, which often includes a mixed bag. You see, I have finally come to understand that God, or whatever force or entity you pray to and take comfort from, does not play tricks. I believe that He, She...It... simply responds to the most consistent vibration or frequency your thoughts or prayers emit. When you affirm truly and confidently, knowing and believing that that which you pray for or choose to create as your experience is not only possible, but is already yours in some fashion somewhere in the universe, just waiting for you to claim it, it ***will*** show up.

It is written that Jesus said that we are to have life and have it more abundantly. When we fail to do that, I think ***that*** is a sin. The truth is that ***sin***, as ***defined*** in the original translations of the Bible, means *"**to miss the mark**."* When we continue to live a life of lack, believing that is what God or the Universe requires of us, we have missed the mark. What are we waiting for, the proverbial pie in the sky? A more encouraging view of sin might be this acronym: S.I.N. meaning ***Someday Is Now***! Life is not a dress rehearsal.

OK, I am reading your mind again. You want to know if I am so darn smart, how come I don't already have in my life ***all*** the things I want. How do you know I don't? OK, I don't. Not yet. And the answer is simple. Remember what I said in the introduction? Ah, don't tell me you still haven't read the intro! Well, if you didn't, I will repeat what I said: ***"We teach best what we most need to learn."*** A quote from the book within Richard Bach's wonderful book **Illusions: The Adventures of a Reluctant Messiah.**

41

The truth is that the laws of the universe work all the time, but since I have not sprouted my wings yet, I am still more human than divine. Well, I could offer a few testimonials to the contrary! (She says with a giggle.) But I digress. (**Warning**: Run-on sentence coming.) When I falter and don't keep my consciousness high enough, consistently enough, when I don't hold a clear intention, if I just don't clearly *know* what I want, or if I hang on to an underlying fear that I can't have what I want or that it will never happen, I allow the world to be too much with me and fear overtakes me. Fear is our biggest enemy. It creates doubt, grips us hard and grabs a hold of our dreams, rattles them in its cold hand and rolls them out like dice...and the universe is compelled to give us a random sampling of some of what we sort of want. But I tell you this....when I do hold a clear intention, am consistent and sure...when I KNOW with a passion that the thing is MINE, I do manifest that which I want. When we are in sync, when our mind, heart, soul *and gut* are aligned, the world is, indeed, our oyster. Proof positive is the fact that you are reading my book and I am now doing for a living that which I love to do.

AFFIRMATION PROCESS

Create an affirmation about something you want to manifest in your life.   Let it be one sentence and in present tense.   Steer clear of saying "I want..." or "I am going to...."   Instead, say "I have...." or "I am..."   Write the affirmation.   Say it out loud.   Wait a moment, and then write down your self-talk in response to it.

Example:

Affirmation: "I am happy, I am healthy, I am wealthy."
Self-Talk: "Sure. I'm a blithering idiot...suddenly cured and rich!"

Write the affirmation again. Say it out loud. Write whatever back-talk comes up next. Do that a few times. Then remind yourself that you are speaking the truth in advance. See yourself happy, healthy, and wealthy. Really get into it. Feel it. Imagine yourself in a year looking happy and healthy, spending money without a care in the world. Believe it.

AN AHA MOMENT

A kindergarten teacher was observing her classroom of children while they drew.
She would occasionally walk around to see each child's artwork. As she came to one little girl, who was working diligently, she asked what the drawing was.

The girl replied, "I'm drawing God."

The teacher paused and said, "But no one knows what God looks like."

Without missing a beat, or looking up from her drawing, the girl replied, *"They will in a minute."*

CHAPTER 8

"Surrendering the How"

© May 2004

Surrendering the HOW
sounds like an easy task
not too much to ask;
Surrendering the HOW...
but can I do it NOW?
I am THAT I am,
A part of the Great I AM,
and I think I can...
surrender the HOW, that is,
if it's not a scam.
Would you like to?
Are you psyched too?
Do you want to surrender the HOW?
Let's take a look, friend.
Noses out of books then,
and find the place of WOW.
WOW, the capital of OZ,
I wouldn't lie; it was;
stands for World of Wonder!
Bolts of lightening...please!

Now the sound of thunder!
WOW is where all the HOWS,
once surrendered, live.
It's where we self forgive.
Are you interested in
surrendering the HOW?
It would mean less worry,
less having to hurry,
and less being sorry.
I do not like to worry.
I do not like being sorry.
Sorry.
"But I want to know how
things could possibly work out!"
I hear you jump and shout:
"GOD, GIVE ME SOME CLOUT?"
OK. I would like some too.
CLOUT, that is.
I don't need to be a wiz,
but I would like not just a little,
for having just a piddle,
would be like playing a fiddle
while Rome burns...yada yada...
and will not help me solve the riddle.
What riddle?
Surrendering the HOW, of course.
For while it sounds like giving up,
it's a veritable Living Cup,
the proverbial and valiant white horse.
"Surrender the HOW?" you say.
"I'm not a quitter,
just a dream sitter,
waiting for them to hatch."
Is it so hard giving up the struggle,
or is it admitting you're a Muggle?
Ah, therein lies the catch!
I want some Harry Potter magic!
Get rid of all life's static.
Have all things democratic;

but I would not,
I could not,
wave a magic wand
and all my cares be gone.
You might say, "I'd like it."
But you would soon see
you'd miss having the satisfaction,
the sense of responsibility.
For while we say
we'd like all our problems solved,
and, at that, in a jiffy,
the thought of losing all the glory
of telling our own little story
sounds just a wee bit iffy.
Surrendering the HOW
isn't selling out the sacred COW!
It's saying...I trust
because I must
or I'll ever be in the dark.
And being in the dark
is no picnic in the park.
In fact, I'd say it's rather stark.
I want multi-colored socks,
I want to out-sly the clever fox.
I want to live outside the box.
I want to hop on a train of thought
and not have it be for naught.
Surrendering the HOW...
Ah! I get it now.
Do my thing.
Don't forget to sing.
Take out life's sting
by removing fear and doubt.
Know that no matter what I see,
the best is yet to be,
and that my higher Self
has it all figured out.

Surrendering the HOW is simple enough once we truly grasp what that implies. It is the process by which we stop worrying about "how" we are going to have what we want, do what we want, become who we want to be in the world, and just begin it.

Surrendering the HOW is, perhaps, most simply a matter of getting out of our own way. Some call it "letting go and letting God." The dilemma that poses for many of us is that we feel the need to be in control. We get an idea to do something different or wonderful. We get all excited and are certain in that instant that we are capable of accomplishing it, and then suddenly we are stopped dead in our tracks by this one question: HOW IN THE WORLD WILL I EVER PULL *THAT* OFF? The irksome, burdensome HOW has reared its ugly head.

We start to wonder and systematically come up with numerous ways we cannot possibly do it. We put so many roadblocks in our own way that we can't imagine how we ever even thought we could have done it. Amazing aren't we? Before long we have bullied ourselves into submission by the tampering, hampering HOW.

Or, perhaps, our brain, moving swivel-eyed, darting here and there, searches for the answer to HOW it can be done, and transfixed, we manage to formulate a plan. Step by step...we are proud and proclaim, "This is how I will do it!" Then weeks, months, perhaps, even years later we lament that our "hows" became cement, and we never got the thing done at all.

Hunched over now, like a hulking giant, our frazzled, fizzled out brain wonders how we could have been so off the mark. However, or should I say "how" aside, when we learn to trust the process of life and believe that the Universe is conspiring on our behalf, we can surrender the "how," and just take action in the direction of our dreams.

Oh, of course, this may include setting some goals for the actions we need to take, but we won't be stymied if we suddenly have to take a detour. Why? Because we inherently know it will all work out for our highest good. Go on now, hold a consistent intention, surrender the "how," take a deep breath of life and say, "I don't have to know *how.* I surrender the *how*, knowing all of this and more is possible."

SURRENDERING-THE-HOW PROCESS

Summarizing: Too often we no sooner think of something we would like to do than a hundred reasons pop into our minds telling us why that very thing is impossible to do or have. We begin asking ourselves HOW that could possibly come to pass. HOW could *that* ever happen to ME?

Suggested process: If you didn't have to worry about or even consider HOW certain things might happen, (and, of course, you *don't*), what would you want to manifest into your life? What would you attempt to do, be or have if you were not so weighed down by worrying HOW in the world you would ever be able to do, be or have *that*? Write some of those things down. Make a list of things. Go crazy. Say out loud: "I don't have to know how. I surrender the HOW, knowing all of this and more *is* possible."

Example list:

- Go back to school and get that degree!
- Find work I love.
- Learn to play an instrument.
- Make new friends.
- Meet someone special.
- Start that book!
- Finish that book!
- Learn to skate.
- Buy a motorcycle.

LAUGH OUT LOUD MOMENT

HOW!

The Lone Ranger and Tonto went camping in the desert. After they got their tent all set up, both men fell soundly asleep. Some hours later, Tonto woke the Lone Ranger and said, "Kemo Sabe, look towards sky, what you see?"

The Lone Ranger replied, "I see millions of stars."

"What that tell you?" asked Tonto.

The Lone Ranger pondered for a minute then said, "Astronomically speaking, it tells me there are millions of galaxies and potentially billions of planets.

Astrologically, it tells me that Saturn is in Leo. Time wise, it appears to be approximately a quarter past three in the morning. Theologically, it's evident the Lord is all-powerful and we are small and insignificant.

Meteorologically, it seems we will have a beautiful day tomorrow. What does it tell you, Tonto?"

Tonto was silent for a moment, and then said, "Kemo Sabe, how come you Lone Ranger and I am lowly sidekick when you dumber than buffalo chip? You want know what seeing all those stars mean to me? It mean someone stole tent."

Chapter 9

Life, the Supreme Juggling Act!

In the throes of moving
the shambles of my mind,
in order to rearrange the order,
to my dismay I find,
as I wear away the rind,
the more I rearrange,
the more disorder.

Juggling is the art of keeping two or more objects in the air at the same time by alternately tossing and catching them. One can juggle with balls, bowling pins, scarves, knives, fruit, any number of objects. The objective is to toss the items in such a way that a pattern is formed, and, oh, yes, to do so without dropping any of them. To juggle successfully, at least one of the items has to be up in the air at all times. Novice jugglers use a varied number of the same item, as their weight is the same and the juggling is easier. More professional jugglers, rather than using all balls, for instance, often use different objects, of various weights and shapes, which changes their speed of descent. The difficulty or challenge thereby increases exponentially, and their superior skill becomes more evident.

The metaphor of juggling objects and juggling life is obvious. In life we juggle lots of things at the same time, sometimes to the peril of one or more of them. Sometimes we juggle things as if they have equal value to us, like juggling balls or oranges, but in reality the things we juggle are not valued equally, yet we sometimes treat them that way. We juggle work, our home life, recreation, personal growth, our social interactions, spiritual pursuits, picking our noses, scratching our butt, stuck in a rut. Oh, my! Too much to *do*. Too little time to *be*.

We determine, or choose, what we hold in our hand, or, more precisely, what we give our attention to in every moment, and what we toss up or leave up in the air.

"The trick to juggling is determining which balls are made of rubber and which ones are made of glass." – A. Nonymous

Being out of Balance

The purpose of juggling, when it pertains to our lives, is to be *in balance*. We can't do everything at once. We can't do it all and certainly not at the same time, so we allot a certain amount of time to one thing over another. One of the ways our lives become *out of balance* is when we let important things fall away because we've lost sight of them while juggling what seemed more immediate, though, admittedly, not more or even as important.

What happens in our lives is a natural result of the choices we make; more often it is the cumulative effect of the choices we've made, so we seldom see a direct correlation. When we juggle things in our lives, unlike the professional juggler of objects, it is more imperative that we not let certain things fall away or allow others to remain in the air too long.

Being out of Integrity

Another way we become out of balance is when we are *out of integrity* in our lives. We are out of integrity when the distance between who we say we are, who we *believe* we are in the core of our beings, and how we represent ourselves to the world is too great. For instance, we are out of integrity when we remain in a job or a relationship that requires that we compromise our values or our sense of self in order to maintain it. Eventually that wears us down, pares us down, until we neatly put our true selves in our pocket and live a life of pretense, a life of *quiet desperation*. It usually happens slowly, insidiously, without our conscious awareness, and then one day we wake up feeling withered, smothered, disillusioned, out of pace, and out of place. When that awakening happens, we have a choice to make. We can go back to sleep, or we can finally give proper attention to all the things in our lives that truly matter to us. We have to ask ourselves some vital questions. Where am I putting my energy? What is it I truly want to do? Who is it I want to be in the world? Perhaps most urgently, where is the joy in my life?

In an article I read by Steve Goodier, entitled "All the Joy You Need," he quoted Thomas Aquinas: "No one can live without joy." True enough and yet, as Goodier points out, while people cannot avoid pain in their lives, they can, and often do, avoid joy. Sounds like a foolish plan to me, but we've all seen those people; we may have been or still are one of them. Such people become so weighed down by their problems, large and small, that they cannot allow themselves to be joyful for even a moment. Their focus is narrow, their concentration is intense. They see only the pain, only the rubble, only that which is in ruins.

Goodier insists that there is joy amidst the rubble of life; laughter amongst its ruins. He is right, and all we have to do to see it, is become mindful of it. We have to look for it consciously. We have to seek it out intentionally. (You can sign up for Steve Goodier's free email newsletter by going to: http://www.lifesupportsystem.com/)

To put our lives more into balance, to put some joy into our days, we have to stop, reassess and manipulate time and space into a more pleasing, more life-affirming pattern. We have to learn to juggle more consciously, more effectively.

My word is my bond. It's an expression we seldom hear these days; it's reminiscent of a time long ago when it was more common to take a person at their word, when a handshake was a time-honored contract. It seems harder now to trust people. After pondering why, my suspicion is that it has to do with our inability to trust ourselves. It is generally a lack of self-trust that renders us unable to trust others.

When we don't trust our own feelings, we fail to nourish our soul, and when we ignore our desires in order to accommodate the wishes of others, we are committing the worst kind of self-betrayal. Some call it self-sacrifice and defend it as a noble and righteous way to be, but just look at that expression: *Self-Sacrifice*. It sounds downright medieval. I'd rather spell it *mid-evil*, for when we turn against our true nature, we are creating at least a mini monster, for we no longer live - we just exist. It's as if we pulled on the word live until the "e" wrapped around to invert the word and create the new word evil.

We are so *out of integrity* with ourselves when we neglect the stirrings of our own heart to avoid the disapproval of others; when we put ourselves consistently in our pocket for fear that what we desire, or how we really feel, will disappoint others. When we do that, we are creating a whirlwind of internal unrest. Soon we become unable to tell the truth even to ourselves. We become estranged from who we really are. We literally become a stranger to ourselves, and often become depressed, which is essentially *anger without the enthusiasm.*

When we don't trust people with the truth, we are telling those we love what Jack Nicholson's character said to Tom Cruise's character in the movie, "A Few Good Men." We are telling them, *"You can't handle the truth."* What message does that give people? How can there be trust without truth?

Yet we're all guilty of it to one degree or another. We all withhold.....just a little.

On the surface, being a person of integrity seems to go hand in hand with being honest, yet a person of integrity, if they are truly being honest, will sometimes not be able to keep their word. That's just a fact of life. Admittedly, it can be inconvenient or even hurtful when someone breaks their word to us, when they fail to keep faith with an agreement we've made, from something as simple as meeting for lunch, to something as serious as renegotiating the terms of an intimate relationship.

Life is uncertain, and even with the best intentions, if we live wide-open and full lives, breaking our word will sometimes be necessary because *change is inevitable.* Part of building supportive and sustaining bonds of trust is being open to the possibility that, with the passage of time, agreements or arrangements may need to be reworked, revamped, reassessed and renegotiated. I used to be a slave to sticking with the original plan. I would feel let down and heartily disappointed if someone backed out the last minute, or if, for whatever reason, we were unable to do what was originally on the map to do. If I were the one who created the need for a change in plans, I would feel awful, even irresponsible. Now I see how foolish that was. How much easier life is when we can simply go to Plan B, and without guilt or recriminations. Why, these days, I've been known to go to Plan C and D too.

I think more heartache has been caused by a failure to be honest, than by speaking the truth, whatever it is. In the name of thinking we are protecting someone by not acknowledging that something has changed, we do them and ourselves a disservice and an injustice. We are so frightened by the possible consequences of being our authentic selves in every moment that we start to ignore those inner stirrings altogether, or we fail to share what truly matters with those we care about; sadly, when we do that, ***the blanket of our integrity begins to unravel***. So, in all honesty, a person of true integrity is someone you can count on to level with you in the moment. What you see is what you get. You don't have to second guess them, because you can trust that if there has been a change in what is possible or how they feel, they will tell you.

We also betray ourselves when we maintain, against all internal evidence to the contrary, that we want what everyone else wants, or what everyone else says we should want. We betray ourselves because being different or initiating change is sometimes frightening. But if we don't meet the truth head on, it will eventually find us anyway, and by then we are likely to be disillusioned at least, and, at worst, broken—and wondering why.

This is what Oriah Mountain Dreamer says about betrayal in her book and poem of the same title: <u>The Invitation</u>:

I want to know if you can
disappoint another
to be true to yourself.
If you can bear
the accusation of betrayal
and not betray your own soul.

(By Oriah Mountain Dreamer from her book, THE INVITATION © 1999. Published by HarperONE. All rights reserved. Presented with permission of the author. www.oriah.org)

I am not encouraging, let alone advocating, breaking your word lightly, in a cavalier manner, not at all. I do believe, nonetheless, that you must be honest with yourself in determining when and where you may have to break a promise in order to remain true to yourself. Sometimes it's a matter of what is at stake. Not keeping your word just because it suddenly seems inconvenient is not good for your soul and will not make your way in the world pleasant. When the thing you promised to do is vitally important to the other person, and it does not go against your spirit, it is a small sacrifice to keep your word even if you are exhausted and it will really tax you. However, if keeping your word is to be done only at the cost of surrendering a piece of your soul, you must give yourself permission to reconsider.

Sometimes, in order to continue growing, you must move to the place where uncertainty and freedom become friends.

While feeling **sure**, feeling **certain** about anything, may provide a kind of comfort for some, especially about the existence of God, I think being open, allowing yourself to question your beliefs, is a healthier approach to life. If we are so certain, so absolute about things, we lose our perspective and our capacity to be *tolerant* of the differences of others. I have an issue with the word *tolerant* though because tolerance implies an ulterior superiority at best, while acceptance implies an open reception to the differences of others. Nonetheless, being tolerant is better than being intolerant, and accepting is better still, but when we can get to the place in our heart when we can embrace others regardless of their differences, what a far better, much richer, fuller experience of life we will have.

So, being out of integrity or out of balance creates the supreme juggling act we do in this life, and the greatest juggling act we will ever do is the one within ourselves between the need for intimacy with another (or others) and our own independence. One of the areas of our lives we seldom *schedule* in is time for ourselves. Few people even know how to enjoy solitude. Many, in fact, are scared to death of it. Some people are just not capable of having a positive or meaningful time by themselves, away from others.

If you have not spent much time cultivating a friendship with yourself, perhaps it is time. Would you be friends with you if you were not you and you met you? (I promise that question makes sense. Read it again if you must.) There must be things you like to do or would like to learn about or explore, some of which are solitary endeavors. Make it a regular practice to spend time with you. You may even start to look forward to those times. The most important love affair you will ever have is with yourself. Love you with all your heart and people will be drawn to you.

Once you have established a friendly relationship with yourself, you are more ready to engage in healthy relationships with others. Relationships with coworkers, friends…family…ah, family, *la famiglia*!

I know most of us come from some sort of "dysfunctional" family. Let me put it another way. Few of us come from "Father Knows Best" families. I suppose I have dated myself considerably again, haven't I? But while television situation comedies in the more recent past reflect some of the dysfunction that exists in real families, like *"All in the Family,"* *"Roseanne," "Brothers and Sisters," "Modern Family",* and *"The Fosters,"* those of the 50's depicted unrealistic, *ideal* families. Television shows like *"Leave it to Beaver," "The Donna Reed Show," "Ozzie and Harriet,"* to name a few, made us think that was the way it must be in everybody else's households but ours. These days there is more realism on display both on television and in movies, and we each struggle with our own family demons. The point is that we may have some mending to do and there is no time like the present. As adults we have the option to approach or view a relationship from a new perspective. If we want lives that are more in balance and more in integrity, we can choose a better way of being in the world that will be reflected in our relationships.

Haven't you known someone who did not have a good relationship with their mother, yet when their mother died, they were beyond consoling? Others might have looked on and said, *"What a show that was! They hardly spoke for years, and when they did, it was a screaming match. Now she's drowning in tears."* There is a very good reason for that. It may not be disingenuine at all. Such tears can make perfect sense. When the significant others in our life die, there are no more opportunities for reconciliation. So, while someone may not be mourning the mother who died, they are mourning the loss of every last chance to get it right. That alone is reason to cry buckets.

So, if you are harboring resentments about a childhood that caused you pain, make it a priority to build a bridge. Talk to whichever relative is at the heart of it. Sometimes an awful lot of hurt was caused by a misinterpretation of someone's behavior. Sometimes it was what it was. In either scenario, your soul can be nourished by practicing forgiveness. The forgiveness is for you much more than the other person; and just maybe *you* are the one who must seek forgiveness from yourself and the other for hurtful things you might have done, or kind things you neglected to do. Seek out those with whom you would like to reconcile, and if a healing takes place, great! If not, you know you made a sincere effort and your spirit will be lighter. Again, it is all about striving to understand rather than finding a reason to be right.

JUGGLING PROCESS

Create a non-edible pie, portioning out the different areas of your life. How much time do you devote to family? We all hear about quality time versus the quantity of time. There's some truth to that, but time must be spent truly nurturing those relationships. To be sure, there is a special comfort just being in the same room or same house with a loved one, each of you absorbed in your own activity. However, spending time doing something together as a couple or a family on a regular basis cultivates those bonds.

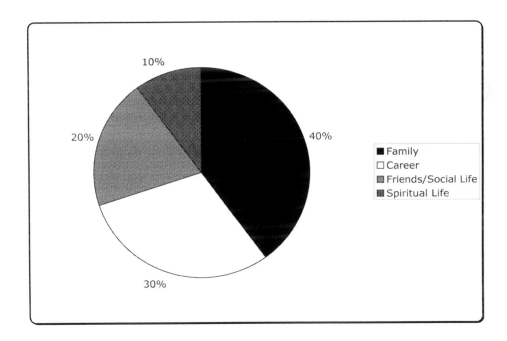

How much time do you devote to your career, to continuing education, to your spiritual life, your social life? Of course, feel free to portion your pie sections with whatever titles best reflect the divisions of your life. First create a pie portioning out the different sections as you currently spend your time. Then recreate it, re-portioning according to your new goals.

Chapter 10

Your Authentic Self

With burning eyes I stare
at faces and forms in flight;
unaware, deemed innocent,
by reason of being ignorant,
they walk by day as if by night.
Each, concerned in their own silent way
with their "society's child" image,
is blind to the images of life that stalk the earth
in search of some out-stretched human hand to understand.
Why do I internalize?
Why must I sensitize every fiber of every feeling
in the fabric of this cell?
Why can't I just ignore
the pounding at my soul's back door
and pay attention a little more
to the chiming of the front door bell?

I would bet money that from time to time in your life you have thought: *"If they only knew the real me, they wouldn't love me anymore."* I have news for you, if *you* only knew the *real* you, you would fall in love with yourself!

If you think you are wonderful, you are on the right track, but for most of you reading this book, you are probably not who you think you are! You are not weak, or stupid, or worthless. You are not a waste of space, or a pimple on the face of the human race. You are not unlovable.

You are a beautiful, spiritual being who chose a human life to experience a variety of emotions and situations. You are courageous, adventurous, and you and your journey have much value. Oh, and, most importantly, you are profoundly lovable.

A Cathy cartoon (by Cathy Guisewite) I once read that has remained with me has four frames. In the first frame Cathy is reminding, encouraging, and chiding her soon-to-be bridesmaids. She tells them there are only four more weeks to get into shape in order to fit into the size dresses they were to wear at her wedding. One responds: "Crash diets are unhealthy and passé." In the second frame she tells them there are just four weeks to tone their tummies and arms. Another responds: "I refuse to conform to society's concept of beauty." In the third frame, Cathy says: "Four weeks until 1,000 pictures are taken of you in one day." In the fourth and final frame, the bridesmaids scatter, alternately shouting, "Run!" "Pump!" "Sweat!" To which Cathy responds philosophically, ***The young work for the mirror. The mature work for the mantel.***

That line got me thinking. The cartoon implied that the young bridesmaids finally decided to get in shape for the "mirror," meaning they were concerned how they will look to others and in the photos, but I saw the line differently; in fact, just the other way around. For me "working for the mirror" means doing not only what makes it easy for us to look ourselves in the eye, or to look in the mirror and like what is reflected back to us physically, but to love who we are as we see ourselves through the windows of our soul. "Working for the mantel" means doing only that which it takes to look good to others, for kudos from friends and family, and/or the world community at large, even at the expense of our own heart's desire. I suspect the former is healthier, but sense the latter is more commonplace.

Do you work for the mirror or the mantel? Do you do things primarily for your own good, your own sake, in response to your own inner stirrings, or to impress other people because you are more concerned about how others will view what you do or don't do, and, will thereby judge your worth? When I ask myself that question, my answer lies somewhere in between. In some arenas of my life I have followed my inner stirrings, and in others I have allowed others to stir my pot.

"Magic mirror, on the wall, who is the fairest of them all?" Most of us are familiar with that line said by the Queen in the fairy tale "Snow White and the Seven Dwarfs." In the context of the story, we understand what the Queen wants to know, but for my purpose here, let's look for a deeper meaning to that questioning of the mirror. What if the word fairest, rather than the general interpretation of the word as the most beautiful, meant, instead, the most just and honest; she who adheres to a standard of rightness, not righteousness? No doubt, some people would consider working for the mirror vain or selfish, but, in actuality, it is merely being authentic and self-loving, being honest and fair with one's own heart's desires.

Oscar Wilde said "To love oneself is the beginning of a life long romance."

My life partner comes closest to working for the mirror than anyone else I've ever known, and I admire her so much for it. She is very talented in a variety of ways, but, unlike other talented people, she is also productive. Hardly a social butterfly, she is, nonetheless, seldom idle. She is either reading, writing in journals, or creating yet another beautiful craft. Her creations, however, are not for sale or even for display on the public mantel. I sometimes think they are worldly manifestations of the decorations one would find on the walls of her soul. There is no vanity in what she creates because she does not care if anyone else ever sees it. Her creations are personal expressions with which she decorates her own environment. She has learned by instinct, it seems, that we all deserve to live in surroundings that nourish us. So, rather than for show on the literal or figurative mantel, her creations are from her and primarily for her. Those of us who are fortunate enough to stumble into her environment are simply happy bystanders who get to observe and appreciate, often in awe, her prolific productions.

In her everyday life, she tries not to do things merely out of a sense of obligation, choosing, rather, to do what comes from her heart. That doesn't mean she never does things she'd rather not do, or that she does not know the meaning of sacrifice, for she still lives on the earth plane. Yet, somehow, she finds a way of living her life, and doing even those things she'd rather not do, with a sense of loving detachment, with a rare knowingness and faith that whatever it is will not go on forever. Then with an amazing sense of renewal, she turns her attention to creating something magical.

So while Cathy of the cartoon says the young work for the mirror, the mature work for the mantel, I don't think whether we work for the mirror or the mantel is determined by our age, at least, not in the chronological sense. I believe it has more to do with our level of spiritual maturity. From that frame of mind, it is the young who work for the mantel, and the spiritually mature who work for the mirror.

How do you peel away those layers that you have added on to mask or buffer, hide or protect who you are from yourself and the world?

Lots of ways:

1. **Choose to go on the most vital, most fascinating journey you'll ever take: THE JOURNEY TO THE CENTER OF YOU**. Once you've made that decision, you'll find the right map. It may be right here somewhere in this book. It may be in another book to which I refer. (Check out the Bibliography.) It may be a documentary that you "happen" to catch on TV, or a lecture you're invited to hear. I recently heard a short presentation by Benjamin Zander. Wow, was it powerful! I subsequently purchased a book he and his wife wrote, **THE ART OF POSSIBILITY**. There's some good stuff in there.

2. **Choose to look at things from a different point of view.** I promise you that Clarence, the angel from Jimmy Stewart's movie, *"It's a Wonderful Life,"* is not going to come down to earth and show you how important your life has likely already been; and it is likely that your life has been important to a lot of people, only you haven't been looking at it through the proper lens. Now is the time, though, that is most imperative for you to make the shift in consciousness that will lift you forever from the land of mediocrity into a world of adventure. Look for what is right and good about your life and dwell on those things. They will expand.

3. **Get excited!** Plan things you can look forward to on a regular basis, and not the same things, but new and different things. Expand your horizons. Make life your own LOVE BOAT. Become your own social director!

4. **Learn something new every week.** Make a list of topics you have always been interested in, choose one a week and look it up on the Internet, or go to the library (they do still exist, don't they?) and research it. Study it. Learn what you can about it, then share what you have learned with someone you think would find it interesting. Once you have gone through your list, just go to a search engine and look for more topics that interest you.

5. **Volunteer your time.** Getting outside ourselves and serving others is one surefire way of overcoming depression. Nursing homes and senior day care centers are always looking for people to come in and present new topics to their residents or clients. Perhaps one of those subjects you have been studying would make an exciting presentation. If presenting a talk is not your thing, just volunteer your time to help serve lunch, or to socialize with the seniors. Listen to their stories. If you resonate more toward children, volunteer at a hospital and visit with sick children, or in the nursery to hold the babies.

6. **Remember you are a Work In Progress!** You may now know yourself better than you ever have in your life. You may be representing to the world more of your authentic

self every day. You may feel you have *finally* discovered who you really are. That is wonderful! Cherish that! Revel in it! But know that same self will change over time. It is inevitable, even desirable. We must continue to grow or something inside us shrivels up. There is always something new to learn, something new to try, something new to explore, something new to achieve, something new to enjoy, something new to love.

AUTHENTIC SELF PROCESS

Which do you work for: the mirror or the mantel? Are you more invested in what others see and how they see you, or in what you see, how you see yourself when you look in the mirror? Do you go about your life truly being your authentic self, your transparent self? If so, explain how in an essay. If not, explain why not.

If you are so inclined and care to, please send your essay to me in an email to: forabetterway@aol.com. Perhaps you would rather share it with someone you feel knows you well. If so, ask them to tell you honestly if your appraisal is aligned with how they perceive you.

LAUGH OUT LOUD ONE-LINERS

I'm the humblest person I know.

I used to think I was indecisive, but now I'm not so sure.

The workshop on procrastination has been cancelled, as no-one got around to enrolling.

Anyone who visits a psychiatrist ought to have his head examined.

There are three types of people in the world: those who can count and those who can't.

The two rules for success are: 1. Never tell them everything you know.

Nostalgia isn't what it used to be.

I'm trying to be less self-deprecating, but I really suck at it.

Once I thought I was wrong, but I was mistaken.

I can be spontaneous, if I have enough time to prepare for it.

I am not in denial!

Being bored keeps me busy.

I don't like to eat. It ruins my appetite.

I used to be a perfectionist, but I'm trying to improve.

All generalizations are wrong.

My apathy causes me problems, but I don't care.

The Psychics Convention has been canceled due to unforeseen circumstances.

Chapter 11

Reaching IN and Reaching OUT for Help

Here I sit, alone, while no one smiles in recognition
or nods in mere cognition
of my presence.
Here I sit, alone, while a flood of faces runs its course,
mindless of my pain, of course,
and I brood about my essence.
Here I sit, alone, accusing those who dare not see.
Amusing, no one's handcuffed me,
yet I withhold myself as well.
Fear and love too commonly dwell
in this same self...oh, what the hell,
"This seat's not taken. Sit with me?"

Sometimes we forget the bountiful resources we have inside us. We are so used to seeking easy answers from things outside of us that we lose sight of the conventional wisdom that dwells within. Just for the record, conventional wisdom is not synonymous with common sense, for common sense seldom speaks of wisdom; in fact, it usually reeks of ordinary, knee-jerk, learned behaviors we have come to believe are correct.

What we require is **un**common sense, the sort of natural wisdom that springs forth from unlikely places, but, nonetheless, resonates within even the most lost souls among us. We recognize it when we see it because it is clearly unbiased, nonjudgmental, simple, all-inclusive, and always comes from love and not fear. The character Edith Bunker, from "All in the Family," was not an intelligent woman, but she had a natural, uncommon wisdom.

It amazes me that we are often more willing to die for something than to live for something; unable to live life fully from that place deep inside us that truly knows.

We dance round in a ring and suppose,

But the Secret sits in the middle and knows.

- Robert Frost -

Some people convince themselves that the answers to all of life's questions are outside of them, out there somewhere. They seek out therapists and psychics to tell them the secrets of life. Seeking help from a therapist or counselor is not a bad or weak thing to do. It can be very beneficial, but we must first go inside, make the attempt, at least, to reach inside for the answers.

When you are troubled, write down your feelings, then ask yourself for an answer, for a solution. Then wait for the answer to come. You may have to sleep on it, pray about it, sit with it a while, but you'll be surprised how often something meaningful and wise does surface.

Psychics may serve a purpose for some, but it isn't healthy to rely on anyone to tell us what to do or worse, *predict* what is going to happen. We tend to fulfill the prophecy; then think the psychic in question is truly gifted. Therapists and spiritual counselors worth their salt guide us inward to discover our own truth.

Reaching out for help can be as simple as talking to a good friend, your mother or father. Perhaps you are close with your minister, sister or brother, a favorite aunt, uncle, or cousin. Sometimes all we need is a sounding board and to know we are loved and supported in all our ways. Growing up I was blessed to have teachers who cared and would listen.

Of course, if what is troubling you is interfering with the natural functioning of your life, by all means get thee to a counselor. Reaching out for help can be a courageous thing to do.

They say it takes a village to raise a child. Perhaps it would be wise to stretch that notion by becoming a part of a community of people we could rely on to sustain us and support us in all our ways. I believe there would be less depression, and certainly less suicides if we each felt connected to something bigger than just our own singular lives and perspectives.

I read a true story about Charles Plumb who was a US Navy jet pilot in Vietnam. After 75 combat missions, his plane was destroyed by a surface-to-air missile. Plumb ejected and parachuted into enemy hands. He was captured and spent 6 years in a communist

Vietnamese prison. He survived the ordeal and now lectures on lessons learned from that experience.

One day, when Plumb and his wife were sitting in a restaurant, a man at another table came up and said, "You're Plumb! You flew jet fighters in Vietnam from the aircraft carrier Kitty Hawk. You were shot down!"

"How in the world did you know that?" asked Plumb.

"I packed your parachute," the man replied. Plumb gasped in surprise and gratitude. The man pumped his hand and said, "I guess it worked!" Plumb assured him, "It sure did. If your chute hadn't worked, I wouldn't be here today."

Plumb has since told audiences that he couldn't sleep that night, thinking about that man. "I kept wondering what he had looked like in a Navy uniform: a white hat; a bib in the back; and bell-bottom trousers. I wonder how many times I might have seen him and not even said 'Good morning, how are you?' or anything because, you see, I was a fighter pilot and he was just a sailor." Plumb kept thinking about that sailor, of the many hours he had spent at a long wooden table in the bowels of the ship, carefully weaving the shrouds and folding the silks of each chute, holding in his hands each time the fate of someone he didn't know. To this day, Plumb asks his audiences, "Who's packing your parachute?"

Most of us have someone who provides that extra something we need to make it through the day. We need many kinds of parachutes as we go through life. In Plumb's case, he needed his physical parachute, but we often need a mental parachute, an emotional parachute, or a spiritual parachute. We all need to recognize when it is time to reach out for these supports to get to a place of comfort or safety.

Sometimes in the midst of the daily challenges life presents, we miss what is really important. I know you have heard the saying: "The devil is in the details," but I think, rather, it is "heaven" and not the devil. The little things, the tiny details matter, yet we often fail to smile and say hello, to acknowledge people, to say please and thank you, to congratulate someone when something wonderful has happened to them, to give a compliment, or just do something nice for someone else for no reason.

REACHING-IN PROCESS

YOUR SPIRITUAL PALM PILOT

Using your imagination, create a Palm Pilot and see it spinning in the palm of your hand. If you don't have a palm pilot or don't know what one is, it's that little gadget used by busy people to keep their schedules, important phone numbers and addresses handy and accessible. However, this one I'm asking you to imagine will not keep your real time appointments for you, it is designed solely to keep your soul's purpose firmly in mind— all those intentions, goals, dreams and desires that reflect your heart's desires. Consult your Spiritual Palm Pilot each morning soon after awakening, and each evening just prior to retiring, and take time during the day to be conscious of it spinning in the palm of your hand, creating a centrifugal force pulling to you that which you have programmed into it.

Although I have never used a palm pilot, curiously, every now and then over the years I have felt an odd itch in the palm of my hand. When I was a girl, I mentioned it once to my mother. She said: "When your palm itches, it means money is coming to you, or you are going to be kissed by a fool." I remember thinking, "What if a fool kisses me and gives me money?" Of course, as I got older I began to reflect on the itching or "I Ching" aspect of all that. Hmmmm – maybe it was just my invisible Palm Pilot being activated!

REACHING-OUT PROCESS

As you go through this week, become aware of the people who pack your parachute, and recognize them in some way. Take someone out to lunch and thank them for everything they have done for you. Send someone a card, saying, *"I may not say it often, but thank you for always having my back."*

If some of those who helped pack your parachute are no longer with you, but in spirit, write them a letter, sign it with just your first name, (for your anonymity), and mail it, addressing it as you like; perhaps, in care of heaven, or the universe, or Italy, or Easy Street...somewhere they always wanted to live. If you feel so inclined, burn it, but whatever you choose to do, even if you want to keep it in a special box, know that your loved one hears your thoughts as soon as you think them, so nothing will be lost.

You may feel the urge to tie it to a helium balloon and let it go, but know that it is not good for the environment, and fragments of balloons can be especially harsh to animals.

Once you have reached out to those others who helped pack *your* parachute, you might want to consider who, in your realm of influence, might be looking to you for help packing theirs. Perhaps you are always there for those people, but let them know, or remind them, that you are, in fact, there for them. If you have *not* been there, tell them that you are and make it a point to be.

LAUGH OUT LOUD

QUOTABLE QUOTES

I've had a perfectly wonderful evening. But this wasn't it.
~Groucho Marx

Coolidge was known for his terse speech and reticence. A woman bet her friend that she could get Coolidge to speak to her, which was something he was reluctant to do.

She went up to him and said: "Hello, Mr. President, I bet my friend that I could get you to say three words to me."

"You lose," Coolidge replied dryly, and walked away.
~Author Unknown

Lady Nancy Astor, Viscountess: "If you were my husband, Winston, I should flavor your coffee with poison."

Winston Churchill: "If I were your husband, madam, I should drink it."

~Author Unknown

Dustin Farnum: "I've never been better! In the last act yesterday, I had the audience glued to their seats."

Oliver Herford: "How clever of you to think of it."
~Author Unknown

The problem with the gene pool is that there's no lifeguard. ~David Gerrold

The trouble with her is that she lacks the power of conversation but not the power of speech. ~ George Bernard Shaw

It's a recession when your neighbor loses his job: it's a depression when you lose yours.
~ Harry S. Truman

When I was a boy, the Dead Sea was only sick.
~George Burns

It's hard for me to get used to these changing times. I can remember when the air was clean and sex was dirty. ~George Burns

I was married by a judge. I should have asked for a jury.
~Groucho Marx

When humor goes, there goes civilization.
~Erma Bombeck

Some cause happiness wherever they go; others whenever they go.
~Oscar Wilde

My wife was afraid of the dark...then she saw me naked and now she's afraid of the light.
~Rodney Dangerfield

Chapter 12

Living a Compassionate Life

A Compassionate Plea

If we but knew another's troubles,
or from whence their heartache came;
if we saw with eyes of mercy,
if we seldom sought to blame.

If we could be a bit more giving
of the benefit of doubt,
we might shed the kind of light
that pushes dark thoughts out.

If we but knew of their beginnings,
or the tenor of their pain;
if we saw with hearts of kindness,
if we seldom thought of gain.

If we could be a trifle wiser,
if we would come from love, not fear,
we might draw to us a paradise,
a piece of Heaven right here.

It is all up to us. It is, once again, about choosing a better way of being in the world.

"You've Got to be Carefully Taught" – is a song with very powerful lyrics that was first introduced in the Rodgers and Hammerstein musical "South Pacific" in 1949. To hear the song in its entirety, go to www.youtube.com and enter the title of the song. Here are the very telling last six lines:

> You've got to be taught
> Before it's too late
> Before you are 6 or 7 or 8
> To hate all the people
> your relatives hate
> You've got to be carefully taught.

****

Children are not born with prejudice and bigotry. Children are essentially open to life and all its experiences, but children are sponges and they easily absorb the attitudes of those around them. If you were one of the lucky ones and were raised by loving, kind, compassionate adults, you have had a leg up. While my childhood was not perfect, I was blessed with kind and loving parents. I am convinced that if all children were raised by people who displayed kindness and compassion in their day-to-day dealings with people, it would act as such a model for their children that there would be no bullies in the world, or, at least, a lot fewer of them. Please know that I am not playing the psychiatric gambit here, implying that all the problems in the world can be blamed on bad parenting; I ***am*** saying that just as children all too often learn to hate all the people their relatives hate, they can learn compassion, as well, by watching ***it*** in action. They can learn not only to be tolerant of the differences of others, but to accept them, and, yes, even to embrace them, thereby making their experience of life all the richer, and by making the world, in general, a better, happier place for all of us. One by one, we each make a choice. Who do you want to be in this world? You can choose a better way of being in every moment.

On some level, we all know that children learn not so much by what we tell them, but by what we show them, by what they see, probably most of all, by ***how they see us acting in the world***. We are not living in easy times. It is not always easy to see the gift in every moment. But there have always been hard times; people will always suffer, and there will always be some pain in our lives. It is our task not to succumb to that pain and suffering. We are the models for the next generations. We must not forget nor refuse to look for the gift in every moment, or we will perish and our children will inherit a negative and somber view of the world and their place in it.

When we hear inspirational or motivational speakers, we might think, *"...it sounds so easy when he says it."* Sometimes, we actually walk away inspired and motivated, for a little while. Then we sink back into our usual routines; nothing seems to change. Some people claim to have *the secret*; others will pay almost anything to get it. When people hear me speak or read something I have written, they often ask me how I remain so positive. Well, this secret, at least, is out: I am not always positive. I remember hearing someone once remark, *"This will never work out,"* only to be reprimanded by a Pollyanna friend, *"You have to be more positive."* *"OK,"* said the negative speaker, *"I am positive this will never work out!"*

Always being positive, kind and compassionate towards ourselves and with others, is not always easy, but the process is *simple*, at least in a philosophical way, once you get the spiritual hang of it. We must choose to reflect in every moment, (before we do or say something, and, perhaps, even when we consistently think something about ourselves and our life), and ask ourselves: *What purpose will this serve? Is this going to help or hurt this person or situation?* It may seem contrived when you first ask those questions, but, I assure you, if you make it a practice, it will become your true nature.

Another practice we can make a part of our life-strategy repertoire is *to look for the gift in every situation*.

When confronted with life's challenges, you can choose to shed some light into the dark corners by searching for the gift, which is the life-affirming option, or you can give up and give in to lesser emotions, which only serve to drain you and pull you farther down.

There have been times in my life when I retreated into books and to writing poetry, living more in my imagination than dealing with the reality of my daily life. While I feel that reading, writing, watching funny or spiritual movies are all positive modes of coping, we have to finally re-engage the world.

Many of us, however, instead of opting for the life-affirming coping mechanisms, (reaching in or reaching out for help), succumb to the illusive, dark and murky world of alcoholism, drug addiction and self-loathing. I have never smoked, neither cigarettes nor pot. *OK, I do smoke after sex....but you have to look very closely.* (Are you smiling?) I have never used alcohol or taken drugs. *My drug of choice at college was Midol!* (Is it still used for menstrual cramps?)

Negativity can be so seductive, and you can easily find someone with whom you can be critical, judgmental and dark. Proving the old adage: *misery loves company*, I suppose. Most of us grew up with a focus more on the negative than the positive. Too few of us regularly heard: *"Don't worry, things will work out fine."* Or *"Don't worry, you'll do great!"* Or *"God will provide."* or even *"I'm so proud of you"* when we were mired in self doubt. The refrains I heard most often were: *"Beggars can't be choosers!"* - *"Stop crying or I'll give you something to cry about!"* - *"Don't count your chickens before they're hatched!"* - *"Do you think money grows on trees?"* - *"It's always something."* - *"When it rains, it pours."* - *"You can't win for losing."* – and my favorite: *"Who do you think you are?!"*

I have experienced several episodes of clinical depression in my lifetime, and even wrote a suicide letter in 1986. The operative word in that sentence is *letter;* had I written the traditional suicide *note*, I might have gone through with it. For once in my life, being prolific saved it; after hand writing eight long pages, I had talked myself out of it.

While on the surface I seemed happy to those around me, and functioned well, I was numbing an inner rage and sadness, keeping my sullen side a secret. The few times that the depression set in and paralyzed me, those closest to me were so thrown by it, they did not know how to help me.

When I was in a healthy space and thinking correctly, I thought I was a pretty special person. The other times, when in the depths of my despair, I wondered how other people managed to *get it* – the *it* that enabled them to have a normal life, a seemingly happy life. It seemed they did not think as much or as intensely as I did, and yet they *got it* without the struggle, without all the turmoil that I required of myself. I thought they must be angels among us.

I have not had a major depression in many years because I have learned to read the signs better. Now when I begin to feel overwhelmed with the old fears and insecurities, born of that hypercritical inner voice that says, "So, you think you're hot shit; well, you're half right!"—I take steps to avoid being pulled down into the quagmire of negativity. By acknowledging the signs earlier, I manage to pull myself out of it sooner. I tell myself what I tell others who come to me for counsel; I remind myself that I am worthy of life's goodness and riches.

No matter how scared and battle-weary you are, claim your power to choose a better way. When things you have tried don't work out, choose a new approach. Commit to being more adaptable, more flexible. Live consciously, with compassion for yourself and

73

others. You have a great capacity to enjoy life and to contribute to the world. Choosing a better way of being in the world is a ***deliberate*** act. It is nothing short of personal revolution. It means discovering who you really are and embracing what you find.

Chapter 13

Be Grateful for Who You Are

I am grateful for a myriad things and for a torrent of reasons. High among them is that I am grateful to be *me*. Somewhere along the way, I finally learned to love myself for who I am and to embrace all the many facets of *me*.

There were times in my life when I picked apart everything about myself. As a teenager, although not overweight, I thought my legs were too heavy. Of course, now I would kill to have them that size! And I had acne up into my early twenties. I would not go anywhere without makeup. I took care of my complexion and even went to a dermatologist for a brief period, but the most important thing I did was decide to make a list of the things I loved about myself and recite it to myself; and not just the physical. I would say: *I love my eyes, I love my hair, I love my smile, I love my sense of humor, I love my good heart, I love my quick wit.* Most mornings I would look in the mirror and say, *I see you, I accept you. I love you.* Sometimes I would imagine scenarios in which people would say, *"Camille, what a beautiful complexion you have."* My complexion improved dramatically over the years, yet I am still surprised when someone compliments me on my complexion. As I may have said elsewhere, I am sixty-six as of this writing, and I have no wrinkles on my face. When people learn my age, they sometimes ask what my secret it. I tell them, good Italian genes, lots of olive oil, and having boobs big enough so that when I take off my bra, they fall and pull out all the wrinkles in my face.

Being grateful for who I am, though, has less to do with what I look like and is more about who I am and how I represent myself in the world. I like who I am, who I have become. I have described myself in a variety of ways, but a while ago I became aware of the phenomenon of being a *Renaissance Soul*, and I have concluded that I *am* one. If you would like to explore whether you are a kindred spirit, check out Margaret Lobenstine's website at: http://www.togetunstuck.com. (You might also want to pick up a copy of her book, The Renaissance Soul.)

This description is taken directly from her website:

What is a Renaissance Soul?

Short answer: A Renaissance Soul doesn't ask, "What color is my parachute?" but rather "What colors are my parachutes!"

Slightly longer answer: A Renaissance Soul has several key characteristics. The first is preferring variety over concentration. The second is that, within that variety, we proceed by widening options rather than narrowing goals. The third is that when the outcome of our process results in mastery and success, we opt for change rather than expansion, to begin something different rather than go on doing more of the same.

I read that and said to myself, *"Woo Hoo...there I am!"* As you read in my introduction, (you *did* finally read the introduction, didn't you?), I am a writer, a speaker, an ordained minister, a standup comedienne, a workshop creator/facilitator in areas of personal, professional and spiritual growth, a performance poet, a pirate, a pawn and a king. I still can't leave those last three out, but, OK, scratch them! I have also been a Hospice volunteer, and a volunteer advisor/trainer/counselor/panel participant in areas of diversity.

I have walked a wide and varied career path. I have always done well in whatever position I was in, and have received comments from supervisors such as, *"She has made the job her own."* Or, *"She has reinvented the position and rewritten the job description."* I have always brought my own spin to the job because I tend to see different and usually better ways of doing things. More than once I have created a new position within a company and filled it. It's not exactly that I get bored doing the same job function day after day (although that is sometimes a piece of the puzzle), and it's not that I have attention deficit disorder, because I can stay with the same project endlessly and focus relentlessly when I am fully into it. My mind just runs a mile a minute in so many different directions that I sometimes make myself so dizzy I can't move at all. A therapist once suggested I might be mildly manic-depressive. I told him sometimes I wish I were, because then I would, at least, have something to look forward to. While I was comfortable exploring, some family and friends around me thought I just did not know my own mind. Now I can say I am just a raving Renaissance Soul! I don't say it as an excuse of any kind; it just helps me see myself from a new perspective. It gives me a better grasp on my life's work.

As a child, I felt like I didn't belong because I wasn't interested in the usual games children played. Lobenstine says we Renaissance Souls are swans among ducks because we don't often fit in, but, truth be told, I always thought of myself as more of an odd duck than a swan. I felt out of sync with family, friends and society in general. I didn't fit neatly inside any box. I preferred to color outside the lines. Whenever I chose a different path, my mother would say, *"Why can't you be like other kids?"* As I got older, and chose to do things contrary to my family's idea of what was best for me, my mother would ask me, *"Who do you think you are, anyway?"* She was not mean spirited at all; she just didn't *get me*, or understand that my wanting something *else*, something *different* from what she had, did not mean I thought what I wanted was *better* than what she had, it was just better *for me*.

As a young adult I could not for the life of me see how anyone could stick with one job their entire working life. My father would caution us, (me, my older brother and younger sister), to find a job and stick with it. He assured us that being loyal to one employer was the only way to have the security of a pension in addition to social security. Curiously, and sadly, after thirty-five years of faithful service with the same company, after working his way from truck driver to general manager, my father was summarily dismissed and replaced by someone half his age at half his salary. The company was sold soon after, and he received no pension. He was bitter about that to his dying day.

In Lobenstine's book: <u>RENAISSANCE SOUL</u>, she explains the difference between a Renaissance Soul and a non-Renaissance Soul. She uses Mozart and Ben Franklin as examples. Of the two, Franklin is the Renaissance Soul, as he had many talents and interests. Mozart knew from a very young age what he was to do, and that is, essentially, what he devoted his life to, beyond anything else. Both kinds of souls can be geniuses or non-geniuses, but, curiously, Franklin reaped financial rewards from his various endeavors, while Mozart died a pauper. Nonetheless, being a Renaissance Soul does not make anyone smarter or less smart, it just determines the way one filters, perceives and, therefore, approaches life and the world at large.

As for me, I either envied those I saw who knew exactly what they wanted and what they wanted to be from a very young age, or I viewed them as cookie cutter replicas of each other, living in the land of mediocrity; not even living lives of quiet desperation because they were content with the sameness, with the predictability of it all. Or so it seemed to me, for I am the one who has more often been desperate, not knowing what to do, where to put my energies.

I understand that my job history confuses some people, and it used to hurt me when certain comments were made. At a holiday party years ago, a former business colleague introduced the friend I was with and me to a third party. She said, *"This is Barbara, she's a social worker, and this is Camille. I don't know exactly what she does!"* And then she laughed. I smiled and said, winking, *"Yes, that's me, a work in progress…or, perhaps, just a piece of work."* I generally use humor to defuse uncomfortable situations. Yet the comment throbbed in my head the rest of the evening, a piercing arrow stuck in my temple. Some years later, at the wake of a favorite uncle, an aunt I hadn't seen in a few years had heard I wasn't working steadily at the time, and asked me, *"You were always so smart. How did you come to this?"* You'd think I was a bag lady!

I subsequently wrote my aunt a long letter, asking her what exactly it was she thought I had *come to.* Was it, I wanted to know, because I didn't have a traditional nine to five job, never formally married or had children? I wasn't really angry in my letter, and, therefore, did not go on the attack. I did not point out to her how miserable she always said she was in her life (especially her marriage). I just wanted her to know that although I did not have an *ordinary* life, I had a happy and very eventful one – for the most part, anyway. I have traveled to seven countries in Europe, to various parts of Mexico, and throughout the United States. More importantly, I have been loved by extraordinary people, and I have loved deeply and well.

I have done many wonderful and worthwhile things. I have worked with abused and neglected children, with people challenged with AIDS, with seniors struggling with Alzheimer's Disease, as an instructor for a domestic violence nonprofit organization, (making presentations to middle and high school students on dating violence and child abuse), as a radio talk show producer and host, as host of a cable TV show, as a standup comedienne, a playwright, a lyricist, an actress, a performance poet. I have been a Hospice volunteer and a volunteer advisor/counselor/instructor of teens in areas of diversity. I didn't mean to go off on a rant there and toot my own horn; I just wanted it to be abundantly clear that no matter what the outward appearance, I have seldom been idle even during those times I was without a traditional *job.* I may not always have had an income, but I was always *employed* - doing volunteer work, writing, providing spiritual counseling on a sliding-fee scale, being me and happy to be a custom-made soul in an off-the-rack world.

.

My dream is to establish a nonprofit foundation, For a Better Way, where, through workshops, presentations and discussion groups, people of all varieties can come together to be encouraged and inspired to choose more wisely how and who they truly want to be in the world. I want to help rid the world of bullying in every arena of life. I want to be able to offer free presentations to schools and organizations on compassionate living, compassionate parenting, and compassionate leadership. With my weekly radio show, *"Tie a Knot & Hang On! Help has Arrived!"* I will have a forum to ignite the fire that will make it happen. My show airs Wednesdays at 1:00 p.m. EST on www.w4wn.com.

Renaissance Soul or not, I hope you are true to your soul's calling.

Be-Grateful- For-Who-You-Are Process:

> *I asked for an apple from a tree in your garden.*
> *Was that too little to desire?*
> *Why, instead of fulfilling a simple request,*
> *did you bid me entrance and show me beauty*
> *until I knew too much of bliss?*
> *Is death to find me surrounded by luxury*
> *yet starving for want of an apple?*

1. What do you think that poem meant? What did it evoke in you? Have you ever felt that way?

2. I wrote the preceding chapter about being grateful for who I am in order to demonstrate what I would like you to do. Although other people's opinions of us are none of our business, write a description of how you think you are perceived by those around you. Then describe yourself and make a list of all the reasons you are grateful to be you. Go on, brag. It can be very nourishing.

Chapter 14

A Conversation with Some Angels
© 1988

I want to reach inside your heart
with words to ease your pain,
to wrap the words around you
so you'll never hurt again.
I want to tell you it will all get better
even though at times my own heart harbors doubt;
I want to mirror your inner beauty
when life's ugliness is all about.
I want to find you the solution,
to be mother, sister, friend.
I want to shed the kind of light
that would make the darkness end.
I want to see you always happy,
to know there's gladness in your heart.
I want to do all a friend can do,
but your soul cries out for more than friendship can impart.
So, I had a conversation with some Angels in the night;
I asked them to work overtime
and this time to get it right.
I told them to explore your soul
to discover what lies there most true,
then to start the heavenly wheels turning
to bring your own true lot to you.
They seemed to smile in mass approval
at the sincerity of my request.
They agreed to do their Angelic part,
but said you had to do the rest.
I said, "Tell me...she is willing
to do whatever it takes to receive
all the good that she's been wanting."

They said, "Tell her to believe."
I said, "She does...at least she wants to..."
"Aha, wanting is good," they said, "But now
she must choose to let go of all past hurting
instead of insisting she doesn't know how."
I sighed, "Can it really be that simple?"
They smiled, "As simple as sprouting wings."
I laughed, "That's easy for you to say, you're Angels."
"And you," they said, "are powerful, divine human beings.
The trick," they quickly continued,
"is believing when all hope seems gone.
It's truly amazing what transpires
when faith is suddenly reborn.
It starts the wheels a-turning
and speeds things right along,
lest doubts and fears, worries and tears
stop the flow of your sweet heartsong.
The Guardians among us angels
do our best to cheer you on your way,
and it causes our wings to shudder
when a sudden doubt or fear brings on delay.
We stand there on the sidelines,
silently shouting, 'Hang on! Hang on!
It's right there around the next corner.'
Yet you often quit when you would have won."
I said, "Sweet Angels, why shout so silently
when what you have to say we so need to hear?"
They shrugged shoulders and wings together, saying
"We are empowered to inspire, not to interfere.
You must learn to listen to the whisperings of your soul,
especially when pain is shouting to be heard,
and to be aware that you attract or push away your good
by your most consistent thoughts and words.
These are not new ideas to such as you,
for in the Soul all are equally wise.
Be gentle, love yourself,
become the one who does, and not who merely tries.
And you dear mortals try so hard
when all you have to do is be

faithful, persistent, full of joy and love,
especially in the face of the things you see."
I thanked the Angels; they embraced my heart,
and together we offer these words to you:
KEEP ON LOOKING FOR THE BEAUTY AND LET YOUR HEART SMILE.
IT WILL ALL BE YOURS IF YOU BELIEVE WITHOUT CEASING.
PLEASE DO!

In November of 1988 I wrote, perhaps channeled, but at the very least, collaborated with the angels on, the poem you just read. I had been up all night, sitting vigil over a suicidal friend. Her nineteen year old son had been in a near-fatal car wreck and had just recently come out of a three-month coma. The prognosis was not good. His spine and his brain were severely damaged and he was paralyzed. His cognitive level was uncertain, but likely to be that of a child of eight, they estimated. The investigation of the **accident** was inconclusive. No other car was involved. No alcohol or drugs were found in his system, yet there were no skid marks to indicate any attempt to brake. It was, therefore, determined that it was either a suicide attempt, (as he had been very depressed), or he had fallen asleep at the wheel. In any case, he had driven off an embankment, and the car had rolled over a number of times.

My friend and I had just spent another day at the rehabilitation center with her son. He could make sounds, but was unable to speak, yet he was able to smile, which he did a lot. He seemed happy all the time. He could move only his left hand and arm, and we had worked out a system with him where he would make a thumbs-up signal to indicate yes, and thumbs down for no. When we arrived at my friend's apartment, she asked me to come up and visit a while. When the elevator opened on her floor, her live-in boyfriend, suitcase in hand, was about to enter it. He said he was sorry, but he couldn't take the drama and the time she was spending with and on her son, so he was moving out. It had been a long day, and his abrupt leaving wore heavily on my friend's already fragile state of mind. She calmly watched the elevator doors close. We walked to her apartment, but she suddenly became frantic and could not get the key in the door. I took the keys from her and let us in. She began to cry uncontrollably, and, finally, threatened to get in her car and do what her son had done.

What do you do when someone threatens suicide? I tried to comfort her. I said her son needed her. I said things would get better. I said suicide was not the answer. I said she had so much to give and would be sorely missed. I said I would be there for her. I said God would see her through it. She finally calmed down and I ran her a bath. I prepared a light dinner for us while she was soaking in the tub, but, understandably, neither of us could eat much. I had planned to leave once we returned from the rehab center, but decided to stay the night…just in case.

I helped her get into bed, turned off the lamp on her night table, left the door ajar and sat in the living room. I fought off sleep, for fear she might get up and do what she had threatened. I found a book and tried to read to distract myself, but tears would come and make that impossible. I kept asking myself what I would say to her in the morning that I had not said the night before. ***What could I say that would make a difference?*** About seven-thirty the next morning, likely in an altered state of consciousness from lack of sleep, I prayed for the right words to come to me. Suddenly, words were coming into my head. I felt compelled to write them down. I could hear myself thinking, ***"I want to reach inside your heart, find words to ease your pain….to wrap the words around you so you'll never hurt again."*** I knew it was the answer to my prayer. I found a composition book and a pen on her desk and began to write down the words as I thought them. I truly didn't know if the words were coming ***from*** me or ***to*** me, but I almost felt as if the words were veritably being channeled to me from the angels themselves. I produced eighty-two lines in a matter of fifteen or twenty minutes. When my friend awoke, I handed her the poem, told her how it came about, and asked her to read it. She began to read, then started to cry and couldn't continue. I went to reach for the scribbled poem to read it to her, when suddenly I realized I didn't have to read it. I ***knew*** it.

I have been writing poetry since I was in second grade, but I had never had an experience like that, nor have I since. I have also memorized my poetry and given readings, but I have never known by heart any of my poems without making a conscious effort to memorize them. I know I had read the poem a number of times that morning, amazed at its message. How many times I read it before my friend woke up I can't be sure. What I do know is that I had been saying it along with her in my head as she read it. So, I put the notebook down and recited the poem to her, both of us now in tears.

I have been able to recite it by heart ever since. It has proved to be a powerful poem for a lot of people, especially for me. Perhaps it gave you some comfort.

ANGEL POEM PROCESS

Go through the poem again and pick out a few ideas that ring true for you, and a couple that, perhaps, don't resonate quite so strongly. Write down how your life experiences have supported, represented or created the concepts expressed in the poem, or how they have made you believe otherwise.

LAUGH-OUT-LOUD MOMENTS

ANGEL MESSENGERS & GOD'S LETTER

One day God was looking down at Earth and saw all of the evil that was going on. He decided to send an angel down to Earth to check it out. So He called one of His best angels and sent her to Earth to observe for a while. When she returned she told God that things were bad on Earth; in fact, she felt 80% of the people were bad and only 20% were good.

Well, God thought for a moment and decided maybe He had better send down a second angel to get another point of view. So, God called another angel and sent him to Earth for a time too. When the second angel returned, he went directly to God and told Him, ***"Yes, the Earth is, indeed, in decline. The first report was accurate: 80% are bad and only 20% are good."*** God said this was not good.

And God decided to send a letter to the 20% who were good. He wanted to encourage them and give them a little something extra so they could inspire others to be good like them.

Do you know what that letter said?

Oh, you didn't get one either?   Bummer.

=====

Joke

Jack and Jennifer, a husband and wife who had been married for fifty-four years, were in a fatal car accident, and soon found themselves in a place they assumed was heaven. Everyone was dressed in white. Some seemed to be milling around, waiting for instructions or directions, while others were standing in different lines.

Finally, a beautiful young man approached them, instructed the wife to follow the woman at his side, and asked the man to choose which line he would stand in for further instructions. "One line," he said, pointing to the sign at the head of it, "is for MEN WHO WERE HENPECKED BY THEIR WIVES. The other line is for MEN WHO WERE THEIR OWN MEN." With that, the beautiful young man left Jack alone to choose.

When he returned some time later, the young man was amazed to see Jack the only man standing at the sign that said MEN WHO WERE THEIR OWN MEN, while there was a very long line behind the other sign. He walked briskly over to Jack and asked, "Can you tell me what your secret was in life? How is it that you are the only man among all these thousands who is standing here?"

Jack shrugged his shoulders and lamented, "My wife saw those signs when we were first brought in and told me I'd better stand over here."

Chapter 15

My Conversation with God

Need to say, got to say
what's gnawing inside this cavity, my heart.
Have to shout, "HEAR ME OUT!"
But never finish when at first I start.
Watching…watching…
all eyes on me.
Waiting…waiting…
what will they see?

"TOUCH ME, SOMEBODY, TOUCH ME!"
Want to know, need to know
what's screaming at me inside this void, my soul.
Tell me how, tell me now
what must I do to make me whole?
Weeping…weeping,
eyes all red.
Softly…softly…
is God dead?

Have you ever had one of those mornings when you kept talking to yourself? I had such a morning some years ago. At first I felt just mildly prompted to sit down at the computer and write it all out; then I felt practically propelled to do so. Even as I sat at the keyboard, I kept hearing myself talking to myself, giving myself pep talks about staying positive, keeping the faith and all that, but, intermittently, I also sensed someone or some thing talking back to me. I hadn't written anything at all related to this book, or anything else for that matter, in a very long time. My mother's cancer had progressed and my time was spent pretty much between work and helping my sister Rosemary with Mom. Rosemary was Mom's primary caregiver and was a blessing to her. Mom made her transition to the other side in October of 1998.

After her passing, as I'm sure is customary when anyone loses someone that close, I took stock of my life. Just a month after her passing, I resigned a position after six years of employment and took that empty-handed leap of faith into the void. Actually, it was not quite so empty-handed, as there was much in my life for which I was grateful, and I was, more or less, keeping my consciousness high, knowing, or, at least, trying to know, as in *believe*, that a wonderful job where I would give wonderful service for wonderful pay was already mine even as I searched for it. I say "more or less," for I felt full of confidence one moment and then, suddenly, the next, I felt fear flooding in.

On that particular morning, I kept talking to myself, but it was not truly a monolog, you understand; it was decidedly a two-way conversation. Although I have been beside myself on occasion, I have never been diagnosed as schizophrenic, so I wondered who it was that was talking back to me. I had sort of figured out by then that when my backtalk is negative or fearful, it is my ego or my little self talking, and when the backtalk is uplifting and rings of the truth, it is my Higher Self. In that instance, I asked myself if it could be the Grand Pupa, the Big Kahuna, the God who allegedly spoke to Neale Donald Walsh in **Conversations with God: An uncommon dialogue.** I believed much of what I read in Walsh's three volumes to be the truth. More accurately, I wanted to believe it, for I wanted it to be true. My constant question to myself then became, *"If I believe it, why don't I act on that belief in all my comings and goings? I mean if I truly believe that what we think most consistently manifests as our experience in life, if I believe that we actually do create our own experiences in life by what we believe most fervently to be so, why would I ever act or believe in any way contrary to that belief? Why am I only able to do that some of the time?"*

So, I decided to speak directly to God. *"God, I am asking in earnest, and I am seeking an answer. I am seeking many answers, my own answers, and yet, I realize, they are universal answers to universal questions."*

Suddenly, I felt a gust of wind move across my face and my fingers flew over the keyboard. Here is the conversation that ensued:

You are right to ask and have the right to ask, and it is my pleasure to answer you. I always answer you. You just don't always hear me or believe me.

Why, dear God? Why don't I hear you? Why don't I believe when I want so to believe, and to have the peace that comes with that belief? I am so tired of saying I believe, only to then watch myself persist in being fearful of outcomes, and, thereby, create in my experience other than what I say I want. I understand the difference between wanting a certain thing or experience of life, and believing, truly believing, that it is possible to have or attract the thing, to manifest it in my reality.

If that were true, if you did understand the difference, you would, as you have said, act on that understanding, on that knowingness, on that belief, always, and you would do, as Jesus did. Your word would be law. There would be no time between your thought and its manifestation.

Then, help me, dear God, help me in my unbelief.

That is the first step. Asking for help from your Mother/Father God. Does that surprise you? My using the term for God that you yourself ascribe to me? It is as true a depiction as any, for I am neither male nor female, yet I am both and more. I am the alpha and the omega, yada yada yada.

Yada yada yada? God says "yada yada yada???" How can I believe that this is You talking and not just my fertile imagination?

Your brother Neale asked the same question. Do you remember my answer to him?

If I remember correctly, I believe you said, "What would be the difference?" Then added something like because you have never thought so clearly or with such wisdom about all these things.

You remember correctly. We are all One. Every creative thought is inspired by me, the One Mind. So, if you are having this thought, it comes from me.

But that makes it sound as though we are mere puppets, with no minds of our own, that we are playing the parts you have assigned for the duration of the play. That's part of what confuses me, the seemingly contradictory notions of predestination and free will. How can I have free will if what I am about to do, say or think is predestined?

89

Why not think of it this way....it is not so much pre-destined, as it is pre-known.

Is that just semantics, like the difference between a used car and a pre-owned vehicle?
Yes. And no.

That clears things up. Thanks. Please explain further.

With your permission.

*With **my** permission? You're supposed to be God!*

And was that supposed to be sarcasm? To answer your question, yes, it can be considered a matter of semantics, but when you lose your wings, my dear children, you seem to lose your balance.

Because a thing is known does not mean it has been orchestrated. Does that clear it up for you?

Not entirely, but I think I know where You're going with this.

I know you remember the angel poem I inspired you to write.

Yes. I can still recite it by heart, all eighty-two lines of it. It was etched into my memory ever since it came out of me...well, inspired by You or the angels in November of 1988.

Then you remember what the angels answered when you asked why they shouted so silently, from the sidelines, when what they had to say you so needed to hear?

Yes, they said they were empowered to inspire, not to interfere. But You're not an angel, You are God. You are the I AM. You CAN interfere!

I can, but I won't because I have given you free will and I will never take that away from you. When you invite me in, I enter. When you seek, I see that you find. When you ask, I see that you receive the answer. But always, and this, perhaps, is the *clincher*, as you might put it: you must always have a clear intent and an unwavering belief to have the thing, find the thing, and receive the thing for which you have prayed. If you waver, the outcome wavers. Not as a punishment, but as a direct result of the laws of the universe as I have established them.

Interesting; that's exactly what I told my father one night; well, actually, it was about three o'clock in the morning. He had awakened with an emphysema attack. I heard him coughing, so I got up and found him sitting at the dining room table. I made him some tea and when his breathing became more regular, we began to talk. He wanted to know why God was punishing him. He wanted to know what terrible thing he could have done to receive such a punishment, to have his very breath withheld from him.

I told him God doesn't punish us; we punish ourselves by what we think and how we think the majority of the time. I shared with him my understanding of thought and the laws of the universe. I said thoughts were like electrical outlets. They can provide positive energy or they can create a disaster, depending on how we use them. If we put the plug to a lamp into an outlet, we get light. If we stick our finger into the outlet, we get a shock. It isn't a punishment, just a natural consequence of our action, according to the law of electricity. I told him I believed it was the same about thought and the laws of the universe regarding cause and effect.

Yes, you explained it wisely and very well.

Sometimes when I am speaking or thinking with what seems to be a higher wisdom, I sense that the thoughts and words are being sent to me or are at least inspired by You.

Anyway, after my explanation, I felt compelled to ask my father a question. I asked him what he would do if Jesus came down right in front of him and said, "John, if you wish to be healed of all your illnesses, all you have to do is forgive all those who have offended, hurt or disappointed you in your life." Through gritted teeth, my father said, "I can't let people off the hook like that." I said, "Dad, don't you see, it's you on the hook, not them? The forgiveness is for you, not for them." He gritted his teeth again and said he just couldn't forgive certain things.

What you told your father was correct. He was simply not ready or willing to accept the truth at that time, but your telling him did plant the seed, and was, therefore, helpful to him on his journey.

So, if I was able to tell my father that truth, why can't I accept it for myself and live a life without dis-ease of my body, mind and spirit?

But, my child, clearly, you can. Sadly, you don't.

OK, then why don't I?

Ah.....you already know the answer to that question even as you ask it.

I do? If I did, I would not be asking it.

I will answer you in the same fashion as I did Neale. OK, you say you don't know the answer, then tell me what the answer would be if you *did* know it.

I thought it was tricky when I read that in his book, and I still think so.

Go ahead. Give it a try. Ask yourself the question and then answer it, believing you know the answer.

OK. Why don't I always act on my beliefs? I don't always act on my beliefs because........because.....because, because, because, because, because, because of the wonderful things he does!

Sorry, I got off on a Wizard Of OZ rant there for a minute. OK, back to my question. I don't act on my beliefs because......

Because I'm afraid to believe it's all true. Because I'm afraid I couldn't keep my thoughts so consistently high anyway. Because I'm hooked on the drama when I don't act on my beliefs? Because if I accept it as true and then slip in my thinking, I would reap an immediate catastrophe of monumental proportions? Because people would make a martyr out of me and come to me to know the truth for them and I would have no life of my own? Because you can't believe it just some of the time, you have to believe it all of the time, and then I would lose my edge, my sense of humor, my sense of the absurd? Because life would become boring, passionless, there would be nothing left to overcome and my life as I now know it would be over?

Ah, then it is not that you are afraid it is too good to be true, but that it is simply too good to be interesting, at least over the long haul. You think if all you have to do is think a thing, desire it with a great and focused intention, the thing is yours...that you would become bored with life? Fascinating!

Fascinating? Didn't You KNOW I would answer that way?

Yes, but I still find it fascinating!

How can you be fascinated by anything if there are no surprises in life for You?

You have finally answered your own question, haven't you? You don't want to claim your God Self because you fear life will hold no more surprises, and, ultimately, it is true, you will be in for no more surprises, as you put it, for you will know everything, have everything, be anything you want to be. But, trust Me, yes, even God uses puns now and again...you will not be bored, my child, for what a grand *knowing* it is.

You will see that it all makes sense, that it is all happening as it should, that even the smallest detail is part of the Divine plan. However, you will not reach this grand knowingness in this one lifetime. There is much for you to learn, much, rather, to experience before that knowingness is fully realized; yet, because there is no time and space in reality, you already know all that there is to know. That is what truly eats at your craw; that is what is at the bottom of all your questioning. You know that you know, for you have shared my wisdom with others on many occasions, and much of your poetry contains that very same wisdom.

I love that you often quote the line Richard Bach wrote in his brilliant book **Illusions**: *"We teach best what we most need to learn."* You are all teachers to and students of each other; yet the truth is that rather than teaching each other, you are helping each other remember who you are, and to rediscover all that you already know.

It all seems rather a complicated game to me. Why all this fuss? Having all these sparks of the divine You out here in countless universes experiencing for You all that You are. It is not an easy concept to grasp. I mean it makes it a little easier for me thinking of God as a Mother/Father God rather than as some supreme Male with a long white beard, sitting on some throne. Actually, that could be one of my aunts. I am Italian, You know. Well, of course, You know. By the way, thanks for the gift of my sense of humor! It has been a saving grace.

You are very welcome. Humor, laughter in particular, is one of my better gifts to the human race.

I agree wholeheartedly, but I'd like to get back to the question at hand. People find it hard to believe there is life on other planets, that there are aliens out there, yet many believe in a personal God. What are You if not a Supreme Alien? Are you some mythical being in charge of all, Creator of it all? Who created You then? Where did it begin? I know...I know...it always was, and always will be, forever and ever, Amen. Truly. Here I am....having a conversation with God. God! G.O.D. = Good Old Determination. That's what I once thought God was. Simply that force of determination, perseverance, stick-to-it-tiveness, the force for good in the universe. That is what I decided You were once I became a Recovering Catholic. Does that offend you?

Nothing offends Me, Child. I don't judge anything. I merely observe and I love you, all of you. Even the ones that you and others judge sinful and or criminal. You are all my children. Oh, and the G.O.D. thing was very clever. Thought so at the time. You see, during that period, G.O.D. was all you could handle of Me. You know very well you have been in and out of what some people call "traditional religion" all of this lifetime. Yet you have always had as your base, as your foundation, the idea of doing good, the highest good for all concerned. That does not, of course, mean that you have always accomplished that, simply that it was your intention, and intention is vital to the soul's growth. Intention for good. One of the most erroneous expressions humans use is *"The road to hell is paved with good intentions."* First of all, there is no hell except the one people create out of fear thoughts, and, secondly, sincere intentions only fall short when they are not sufficiently clear, or when sudden doubts or fears bring on delay or thwart your efforts altogether.

That is another thought expressed in your angel poem. My child, you have always sought answers in earnest, and I have always supplied you with the answers you could accept in any given moment. The trick, as you put it in that same poem, is believing consistently. That is what is meant by praying unceasingly. Holding to your belief even in the face of the things you see...or, rather, choosing to believe in the evidence of things not yet seen. A simple thought to help keep your belief system intact is one you have used and shared with others: Only good comes to me...only good goes from me.

Yes, it is very powerful. I should say it, think it more often. I have seen it work wonders when I have suggested it to others. I'm convinced it changed one woman's life entirely for the good when I was working for the United Way. I was visiting her in her apartment on Miami Beach to see if she were eligible for home care services. Her name was Edna.

She answered the door in a house dress, barely standing straight, moaning and groaning all the way back to her bedroom, where she asked me to help her get back into bed. She was in her late sixties and had suffered a recent heart attack. She was applying for home care as she couldn't go out and do her own food shopping, or even light housekeeping.

Throughout my asking her the preliminary and perfunctory questions in order to complete the requisite forms, she had interrupted me with intermittent statements like, "There is no God, you know" or "If there is a God, He doesn't give a damn about what goes on down here." So, when all the forms were completed, I put my papers down and said, "You seem to want to talk about God, and that is not a part of my job function with the United Way. However, it's just about time for my lunch break. Is it OK if Ms. Sanzone leaves and Camille comes for a visit?" She looked at me quizzically, but then said, "OK." But You know all this, God, why repeat it?

So that you remember the lesson it taught you. Continue.

OK. We talked for about two hours, which put me way behind schedule, but, clearly, it was the real reason I was there. In fact, I'm certain it was the reason I went to work for the United Way, for I was only there for a month, and that was my first week on the job.

I asked her to tell me a little about herself and what her life had been like recently. She said her husband had died of a heart attack six months ago, after forty-four years of marriage. She said everyone had expressed their sympathies, and friends who had lost their husbands commiserated and said they knew how lonely she must feel, and on and on. I asked her what her marriage had been like and she began to cry.

She admitted that she was feeling guilty because everyone was acting as if she should be sad and lonely, but, instead, she was happy when her husband died. In fact, she had felt relieved. Edna's husband had been a silent, brooding, abusive man all of their marriage, and was only nice when others were around, which was seldom because he couldn't abide other people. She said he never had a kind word for her, and would never agree to do any of the things she enjoyed. She said he was very self centered and critical of everything she did or said. I said I could understand why she felt relieved at his passing, but that she certainly didn't appear happy about it. She said along with the relief came a boatload of guilt so she couldn't allow herself to feel happy. She said it just wouldn't be right.

*I asked her if she thought it was possible that her enormous guilt had played a part in bringing on her own heart attack. She looked at me with such amazement and asked, "Is that possible?" I played therapist and turned the question back around on her again, "The important thing is do **you** think it's possible?" Obviously, she did.*

95

Then I asked her what a typical day in her life was like. She recited a generally boring accounting of waking up, taking her medication, making a small breakfast, getting back into bed and resting. She said she couldn't even read or watch television because she would just start crying. She said she would wait by the phone for her son, her only child, to call her, but he seldom did. She said she would wait for a neighbor to call or come by to see how she was or to find out if she needed something from the store, but they never did. I asked how she was with her son when he did call. She said she usually was sad, wound up crying; complaining that he never calls or comes to visit. I asked how she was with her neighbors when she ran into them in the building. She said, "How do you expect me to be? I'm supposed to be a grieving widow, and, after all, I just had a heart attack." Then she looked at me and said, "I guess I'm not too much fun to be around, am I?"

*I asked her what she expected tomorrow to be like, and she said she expected it would be pretty much the same as every other day. I said, "Well, then it will be, but tell me, what would you **like** tomorrow to be like?" She looked at me strangely, but I was on a roll, so I continued, "In fact, what would you like your **life** to be like? What would make you happy right now?" She hesitated. I asked her again. I told her no one would know but the two of us, and encouraged her to be outrageous and just say anything that came to her mind. With a bit more coaxing, she finally responded.*

With a broad smile on her face, she said, "Well, I would like my son to call more often, and act like he wants to talk to me, not like it's a chore or an obligation. I would like my neighbors to call or stop by for coffee and chat a while. I would, naturally, like to feel better, to have my old energy back so I could do some of the things I couldn't do while my husband was alive." I asked what some of those things were. She said she'd always wanted to plant a garden, volunteer at a hospital for children, and take a course at adult education to learn to speak Spanish. Then she hesitated.

I prompted her to continue. She said, "No, that would be expecting too much...." Then she saw the look on my face and said, "OK...OK. I know it's ridiculous at my age, but I would like a man to take me dancing! There, I've said it!"

She said she loved to dance and hadn't gone dancing since she was single. I told her that everything she wanted was possible. I told her it was important for her to change her thinking and that sometimes the best way to do that was to be around like-minded people. I mentioned a group which met in her neighborhood weekly to talk about positive prayer. It was facilitated by a minister of the local non-denominational Science of Mind church.

At first she gave me one excuse after another, saying she didn't drive, she wasn't up to it, etc., etc. I said the choice was hers, but that I was sure if she called the group, they would arrange to have a volunteer pick her up. Then I said, "But most importantly, I want you to do this, without fail. Every night, just before you go to sleep, I want you to write this phrase in a notebook over and over again until your arm gets tired: ONLY GOOD COMES TO ME AND ONLY GOOD GOES FROM ME...ONLY GOOD COMES TO ME AND ONLY GOOD GOES FROM ME. I want that to be the last thought you think before you go to sleep and your fist thought upon awakening. So when you wake up in the morning, before you even get up to go to the bathroom, I want you to take that notebook and write again, as many times as you feel comfortable, ONLY GOOD COMES TO ME AND ONLY GOOD GOES FROM ME, and I guarantee that there will be changes in your life almost immediately."

There was suddenly a sparkle in her eyes. She got up from the bed and retrieved a composition notebook from a dresser drawer; you know those old-fashioned bound black and white ones we used in elementary school. She announced that she would start writing it that very night.

I concluded our visit by letting her know I was approving her for home care and that someone would come to do the shopping for her twice a week, and would do light housekeeping those same days. She hugged me and I left.

I wasn't due to visit her for four weeks, but just three weeks to the day I first met her, she called me at my office. When I picked up the phone, I heard, "Is this my guardian angel?" I didn't recognize the cheery voice, but then she identified herself. "It's me...it's me, Edna, and have I got news for you!"

She went on to tell me that she had just gotten home from a doctor's appointment. The doctor had said he didn't know what she had been doing, but to keep doing it. Her blood pressure was excellent, and he took her off two of the three pills he had prescribed for her.

*She continued. Her son was calling her at least twice a week, because, he said, "Mom, you've been so upbeat lately, you cheer **me** up!" One neighbor had suddenly dropped by, and after a brief, light chat, had invited her to a luncheon at one of the other neighbor's apartment in the building. She said she went and got reacquainted with her neighbors who couldn't believe the change in her. Now one or the other of them calls regularly to see if she needs anything from the store or if she wants a ride to the store.*

She saved the best for last. She said she called the number for the group that meets weekly, and it turned out that a gentleman two buildings over attended regularly and was happy to give her a ride. She had been to just two meetings, but had already learned so many things, and had already started a second notebook, writing ONLY GOOD COMES TO ME AND ONLY GOOD GOES FROM ME. She swore it was magic, because the gentleman who takes her to the meetings had left a message for her on her answering machine that very morning. She had found it when she returned from the doctor's office.

She said, "I memorized the message. He said: There's going to be a dance at my temple next week. I love to dance, but I haven't gone dancing since my wife died ten years ago. Edna, please say you'll go with me." She said she felt like she'd died and gone to heaven. She was bursting with delight, and said she'd never felt better in her life.

That was one of your best moments, Camille. The student was ready and the teacher appeared.

I remember it like it was yesterday. I walked out of her apartment as though I were walking on air. I knew something important had transpired. But I still don't get it. If I know how powerful thought is, why don't I do that for myself all the time? Why don't I act on my beliefs?

You tell me.

Here we go again. I should answer my own question?

I can only tell you what you are ready to hear, and what you are ready to hear you already know anyway.

What I am ready to hear? That old thing about not being able to bring someone out of the cave because the light would blind them?

Sort of. It is just that when someone is not ready, and that is where your free will comes into play, they cannot be made to understand a thing, anything. Watching you, watching all of you, in the day-to-day, even moment-to-moment struggles between choices, and that is what it is, it is all a series of choices, some good, some better, but all are *right* choices, according to what it is your soul wants to experience at the time.

Although, in essence, I know what choices you will make, it is not because I have dictated it so, or scripted it thus, but because I know your heart and I know your mind as it is unfolding, as it is opening. There is only One Mind, and, because there is no real time, no before or after, I know it...whether it is just before or as it happens. Time is just an illusion and you have free will within it so that you can have the fullest benefit from this earth experience. You live in a realm of possible futures, based on the choices you make. You are always free to make your own choices and to choose again, and just because I know what choices you will make does not mean I am any less enthralled or intrigued by them, for you can and often do change your mind at any given moment,

98

surprising even me. Well, sort of. Besides, you watch certain movies over and over again, do you not, even though you know how the story ends?

Well, yes, I do.

Which ones?

I guess the ones that tell me something about life, about who I am, especially the ones that say it with spirit, humor and passion.

Yes. Cinema is a wonderful vehicle through which and by which to be transported to a new plane of understanding. Books, movies, plays. The original "morality plays" served that purpose, although the concept of *morality* plays was a bit heavy handed. Most things are **out of balance** when people insist there is an **absolute** right and wrong of things.

I have a problem with that, too, once in a while. In certain things I guess I think there is a right and a wrong, and in others, there is just a different way of looking at things. Are you saying there are no absolutes in the world?

There is one and only one absolute: that **life exists in order to express love**. Life has always existed and it will always exist, in one form or another, and that will always be its purpose: Love. **Love is all there is.** Everything and I mean **everything** you do, everything that is done in the world by anyone, is **an expression of love or a cry for love**. I never asked that you judge each other, yet so many of you do and say it is done in my name, which makes you feel entitled and self-righteous about it. And that is not a judgment on my part, it is merely an observation. When you are expressing love, it is unconditional and the feeling in your heart is sublime. When you are crying out for love, the action is coming from fear of rejection and often expresses itself in unkind and even violent behavior, pushing away and sometimes destroying the very thing for which you yearn, for you which you crave, for which you are desperate.

"Love and fear too commonly dwell in this same self." Quoting myself, or am I? No doubt, another thought inspired by you. (Complete poem opens Chapter 11.)

Everything you do is out of love or out of fear. Yet even fear comes from love, the fear of the loss of it, or a sense of the lack of it. One who experiences fear in any form, but

99

especially as a lack of love, has forgotten who she or he really is, and, has, therefore, allowed themselves to feel separated from me. I tell you, no one is ever alone or unloved, although many feel that they are both. You are **all** my children; you are all a part of me, and a part of each other.

I know a lot of people believe there either is no God, as Edna did for a moment, or they feel I have forsaken them. I forsake none of my children. I am ever present with them, even as they are ever present with me. There is no free will in this. The only choice there is lies in remembering or forgetting that this is so. Some people say "The sun is not out today." That, too, is false, for the sun is always there. At times, the clouds simply block your view of it. In the same way, cloudy or faulty thinking produces the notion that I AM NOT or that I would choose not to be there for you or any of my children in any given moment. The truth is that I AM THAT I AM and I AM WITH YOU ALWAYS.

I feel I am being prompted to stop our conversation at this point. Until forever then.

Well put, my Child, well put.

CONVERSATION PROCESS

Is there any mythical being, religious person, historical figure, fictional character, deceased relative, favorite author or poet with whom you would like to have a conversation? Get some paper and start the conversation. Take both sides, of course. It may surprise you how easily the words come from this imagined companion. When we do such practices in my workshops, people often ask if we are tapping into cosmic consciousness or just using our imagination. If the message rings true, if it guides, supports or comforts you, does it really matter?

LAUGH OUT LOUD

Bloopers in the church

The following are actual church bulletin board bloopers found in churches across the United States:

"Due to the Rector's illness, Wednesday's healing services will be discontinued until further notice."

"Weight Watchers will meet at 7 PM. Please use large double door at the side entrance."

"Remember in prayer the many who are sick of our church and community."

"The eighth graders will be presenting Shakespeare's Hamlet in the church basement on Friday at 7 PM. The congregation is invited to attend this tragedy."

"A song fest was hell at the Methodist church Wednesday."

"On a church bulletin during the minister's illness: "God is good - Dr. Hargraves is better."

"Potluck supper: prayer and medication to follow."

"The outreach committee has enlisted 25 visitors to make calls on people who are not afflicted with any church."

"Eight new choir robes are currently needed, due to the addition of several new members and to the deterioration of some older ones."

"The choir invites any member of the congregation who enjoys sinning to join the choir."

Chapter 16

Nourishing the Body, Mind and Spirit

Touch me in secret places
where no one has touched me before.
Touch me in sad, silent places,
where saying nothing truly says more.
Touch me in the morning
when night still clings like a sham.
Touch me at twilight
as I begin again to know who I am.
Touch me gently, for I am fragile.
Touch me firmly, for I am strong.
Touch me often...
for I am alone.

Nourishing the Body

Movement, food, laughter and touch – all are essential to living a happy life.

Daily exercise *does* help nourish the body. There, I've said it. Do I *do* it? Well, if *exercising caution* counts, yes, indeed, I do. My strict Sicilian upbringing still clicks in sometimes and I exercise way too much caution. However, the habit of daily exercising has always escaped me. The important thing is that we *move*. We must keep the body moving, and, as I said earlier, I know only too well that when we are depressed, the last thing we want to do is move. We don't want to move out of bed, move off the couch, or move a muscle, let alone take a nice walk around the neighborhood. Dancing, however, if I put on just the right music, is usually a sure thing. Nobody is watching. Go for it!

The trick is to pay attention to your body and to your mood so you can cut off at the pass any deeply entrenched bouts of depression. Unless clinical in nature, depression can be forestalled. Most of us suffer from situational depression, which means our depression is caused by a change in our experience of life and not due to a chemical imbalance. When you first notice a shift in your mood, spiraling downwards, that is the time to do something. Get moving. Take that walk. Play some loud music and dance.

Or we can do some internal jogging: LAUGH. Watch a funny movie that you know makes you laugh out loud. Call up a funny friend who always keeps you in stitches. Go on line and check out one of the many joke sites.

When I was in the depths of my own depression, I used to greet the mornings with *"Good God, morning!"* instead of my usual *"Good morning, GOD!"* The dread one feels in the morning when you are depressed is the worst time of the day. Are you going through that? If you are, change your morning routine. It can be as simple as changing what you eat for breakfast. Try looking in the mirror and repeating: *I am grateful for this beautiful, brand new day!* Even if you are not buying it right off the bat, it will set the intention for and the tone of the day.

Eating well is important. Until I was thirty-five, I could eat anything I wanted and not gain weight. Then my mother's curse took hold and I started to gain weight. I had called

104

off my wedding when I was twenty-four. Twelve years later, out of the blue, I received a phone call from my ex-fiancé. For some inexplicable reason, after catching up with our lives, he asked me if I was still in shape. Since it was clearly none of his business, I said *yes*, laughing to myself as I thought ***round is a shape***.

I remember one particular Sunday morning, December 8, 2002. I woke up praying God would hold me in His grip just in case I slipped off that piece of rope I had knotted and was hanging onto for dear life. I mustered up what little energy I had and grabbed a book from the shelf that I had bought a while ago. I was prompted to buy it because of its title, as you, perhaps, were prompted to buy mine. It was Karen Scalf Linamen's <u>I'm Not Suffering from INSANITY...I'm enjoying every minute of it!</u> I read all 173 pages in one sitting. There was one particular passage I want to share with you. Let me preface it for you first.

Karen was explaining that she had gone through an eighteen-month bout of depression, during which her friend Beth was a godsend. On one occasion Beth came and kidnapped Karen and took her to a movie for therapy.

Here is what Karen wrote:

"Beth is not only a very good kidnapper; she makes a mean casserole to boot. One day she dropped by to cheer me up. She brought with her this heavenly casserole. I mean, this casserole was amazing. It had tons of cheese and sliced eggplant and some eggs and tons of cream, and it had this Mediterranean flavor thing happening, and it just melted in your mouth, and it was truly wonderful.

I get sort of passionate about food, if you hadn't noticed. Anyway, so Beth shows up on my doorstep, and I make us some coffee, and we dig into her casserole, and we spend several hours just talking about life in general and my life in particular. It was nothing short of a Kodak moment, all the encouraging and bonding and feasting that was occurring.

Early afternoon, I walked her to the door. She paused on my front porch, and our conversation began meandering toward good-byes. We chatted casually about nothing in particular, when suddenly I announced, 'I'm going to make it.'

Beth said, 'I KNOW you're going to make it. You're strong. You're a wonderful person, and you've gone through some tough times, but, yes, you're going to make it. And I'm going to be there with you every step of the way. No matter what the future holds, no matter what decisions you make with your life, I love you. I'll be there for you. You're going to be okay, Karen. This year is going to be a new chapter in your life. You're going to be fine. You really ARE going to make it.'

By now there were tears in her eyes.

I blinked. I stared. Then I said, 'I meant the casserole.'

'The casserole?'

'I meant I'm going to make your casserole.'

We got a good laugh out of the incident. But the truth remains that Beth's cooking and her empathy were the perfect combination of ingredients to raise my spirits and put a smile on my face."

I loved that story! I heard laughter and suddenly realized it was my own. I was actually laughing out loud, probably for the first time in weeks. Of course, then I cried. Laughing, crying…both are great releases.

There is a poignant scene in the movie *"Steel Magnolias"* when Sally Field, whose character's daughter, played by Julia Roberts, has just died. Sally is walking in the cemetery with her close friends, played by Olympia Dukakis, Dolly Parton, Daryl Hannah, and Shirley McClaine, whose character's name was Weeza. Weeza, in case you haven't seen the movie, is an ornery old woman with a sour disposition most of the time. Anyway, Sally's character is screaming at the unfairness of it all, wailing that no mother should have to bury her child. She is ranting and crying hysterically when she abruptly stops and says "I'm so angry, I just want to hit something…to hit it hard!" Olympia's character instantly grabs McClaine's character and shoves her in front of Sally, saying, "Here, hit Weeza!" After a very brief pause, they all burst out laughing…except Weeza, of course.

The entire movie audience went from sobs to guffaws in a flash as well. I love when that happens. Of course, the opposite often happens too. It is all good.

Karen's anecdote about her friend Beth and the casserole illustrates a couple of things: Nourishing the body with food and nourishing the body with laughter.

Eating and laughing, (although I caution you not to do both at the same time, or you might choke!), shift and create chemicals in the body which promote and even accelerate healing. The obvious benefits of eating healthy food need no further discussion here, but it is also true that eating food which has been prepared lovingly for you or by you (the preparing of which is therapeutic in and of itself), is also beneficial. That is why we call it *comfort food*. Please understand that I am not encouraging you to use food as your drug of choice. Truth is I am still working on nourishing my body with more than food and laughter. I was serious when I told you near the outset that *we teach best what we most need to learn.*

Indulge me. Here is another story about food and laughter. My mother, may she rest in pizza, (believe me, she would love that!), was not a funny person, but she did and said things which we found funny. One particular Sunday, a bunch of us descended on my mother's house. Mom, unlike most Italian women of her generation, did not like to cook, although she was a fairly good one. In any case, she did not like unexpected company, especially at dinner time. So, as dinner time approached, I checked out the contents of my mother's refrigerator and suggested we all help to make chicken soup.

I assigned the tasks. Mom got out all the fixings, my sister cut up the chicken, my cousin cut up the vegetables...you get the picture. My job was putting it all together and seasoning the soup. My final touch before adding the orzo macaroni is adding about ¼ cup of fresh lemon juice, and dropping in halved pieces of corn on the cob the last twenty minutes. In order to strain the juice of the lemon into the pot without getting any pits in it, I asked my mother for a cheese cloth. She said she didn't have one, and gave me, instead, a large white man's handkerchief, neatly folded and ironed. It worked fine. Later, as we sat down to eat, I said, *"Isn't this nice...we each helped in some way to get this delicious soup on the table. Even you, Dad. We used one of your handkerchiefs to strain the lemon juice."* My mother quickly interjected, *"It was NOT your father's handkerchief, it was the handkerchief I put in the crotch of my girdle to keep it clean."*

Chicken soup spewed all over the table, as we laughed hysterically, tears rolling down our faces. Mom did not see what was so funny. She indignantly said to me, *"You had no problem thinking your father had used the damned handkerchief to blow his nose! What's the difference? It was clean, wasn't it?"*

107

Food…glorious food! Sometimes we reach for food when what we are truly hungry for is *touch*. Being touch hungry is common when we are depressed, when we are without a life partner, when we have a distant life partner, when we get older, when we are sick, when we are away from loved ones for whatever reason, or are simply alone. Sometimes we may even live in a house filled with people who love us, but are still touch hungry because nobody thinks to hug each other unless somebody leaves the house for any extended period of time. Whatever the scenario, too many of us don't get touched very much at all. In my poem which opens chapter 13, one of the lines is "TOUCH ME…SOMEBODY TOUCH ME!" We don't touch or hug each other nearly enough.

I have worked with seniors in a nursing home environment and a day center, and I know just how touch hungry they can be. Having lost their spouses many years ago, those around them don't realize that nobody touches them anymore except to provide personal or medical care. Always respectful of boundaries, because not everyone is receptive to a hug, I would learn over time which of my lovelies, which is what I called my seniors, wanted a hug or simply enjoyed having their hand held while we spoke. When I worked with people challenged with AIDS in the eighties, I would tell them I always had my arms with me and they could come get a hug anytime. Most people were afraid to touch them, let alone hug them.

I loved the Diana Ross song: ***"Reach out and touch somebody's hand…make this world a better place if you can…."***

Still, laughter may, indeed, be the best medicine.

NOURISHING-THE-BODY PROCESSES

When we nourish the body, we nourish the soul, and if we are mindful, we nourish the brain, which nourishes the body. If we eat healthy food, we nourish our body and brain, and if we eat deliciously, we nourish the soul!

For your enjoyment, (not necessarily, your health), I have included some of my own recipes in the appendix in the hope they will nourish you - body and soul.

THINGS WE CAN DO TO NOURISH OUR BODIES:

1.   Schedule regular massages and share foot rubs with someone you love!

2. Exercise daily for at least fifteen minutes
3. Dance often
4. Walk (And whenever possible, walk in pretty places, near a lake or trees, taking time to breathe in the beauty of nature; don't just walk at a fast clip.)
5. "Find yourself somebody to love!" They're not just lyrics to a song. Make love! It surely does do a body good…as well as the soul. The mind doesn't mind either.
6. Eat well
7. Laugh often
8. Ride a bike
9. Hug more people and ask for hugs too!

Nourishing the Mind

Love knows no limits,
Love knows only love;
It is the melody of life,
the stuff songs are made of.
Love takes us like an old guitar;
love plays us with a special hand.
The music is sensual and sweet,
the language one we understand.
Love reaches inside us, searching,
touching, moving us to the core.
Love shows us the possibilities;
…it whispers
"Hold on, there is something more."
Love takes us outside ourselves;
love carries us to the farthest star,
then brings us back to look inside us
to discover, at last, who we really are.

Custom-Made in an Off-the-Rack World...

I first heard that expression in an episode of the TV show, "Mash." Alan Alda's character, Hawkeye, said it to Loretta Swift's character, Hot Lips.

They were talking about not being able to find love, and Hawkeye said, ***"Our problem is we want custom-made in an off-the-rack world."***

In a world where we are often expected to follow in our parents' footsteps, or live in a Levitt house, it's easy enough to fall into line and have a cookie-cutter type of life. If that sounds disparaging, forgive me, for my intention is not to demean those who lead traditional lives. In fact, I readily admit that the world needs a semblance of order and constancy, the salt-of-the-earth kind of people that keep the gears moving on the planet.

But we also need the others, those of us who always felt out of step, who never quite fit in, who wondered as children if we had been adopted even though we shared the same nose as our father and half his family. Well, not the EXACT same nose, we each had our own. We need the misfits, if you will, to add flavor and color to our world.

Just because Jane does not want what Joan has—does not mean that what Jane wants is superior to what Joan wants and has. It is not a matter of better than, but ***different*** than.

Many of us who don't fit into off-the-rack clothes, (or lives), often ardently wish we could for a number of reasons. It would be simpler and more convenient for starters. Mavericks of any variety don't have an easy time of it. We unconsciously put such demands on ourselves, forging new ways of doing and being in the world that we struggle without realizing why most of the time. We sense something is wrong, something does not mesh. We don't know what it is, but we are somehow convinced whatever it is—that the something wrong is ***us***, or, at least, is a failing in us.

Those of us not content with the off-the-rack version of life are the artists of the world, the poets, writers, painters, actors, dancers, cooks, sculptors, teachers, intuitive and nurturing social workers and mothers, those unconditionally loving entities with Down Syndrome, on and on. We come in all shapes and sizes, intellects and guises. Our uncommon commonality is that we see life at an angle. We may suffer more than the average person because we feel things more deeply, see them more clearly, sense them more intensely, but we also have a greater capacity for joy for those same reasons. It is an interesting and compelling trade off.

Maybe it is as straightforward as having an allergy to the madness of mediocrity, or, at least, to the sameness we see in the world, which stuffs up the sinuses of our creativity until we are sure we can't breathe.

"They broke the mold when they made him." People say that about people who seem to be one-of-a-kinds. Of course, the truth is we all are one of a kind in our own way.

110

Even cookies made with a cookie cutter are a little different one to the other; we just have to look more closely. And those of us who do buy off-the-rack often add our own flare by removing a belt, or adding a scarf. We each can put our unique brand or view on things.

Christmas – 1950 - Picture it!

My brother Johnny was eight, I was three, and my sister Rosemary was just five months old. Notice how we are each looking in a different direction. I found that so curious when I came upon that photo a while ago! The reason I found it so curious is that although we were raised in the same household, allegedly by the same parents, we have always seen things differently and have very distinct perspectives on life.

What determines our perspectives? How do we form the opinions that ultimately compel us to view life a certain way? I would suggest it is the filter through which we see it, but then what creates such diverse filters? Perhaps it has to do with how we nourish our minds. Perhaps it is just one more of life's mysteries.

I opened this chapter with my poem "Love knows no Limits." The last four lines are:

Love takes us outside ourselves;
love carries us to the farthest star,
then brings us back to look inside us
to discover, at last, who we really are.

Who are you really? Are you your mind, your heart, your soul? We likely know by now that we are not just our bodies. The heart is just an organ. It is not truly the "heart" of who we are. The heart that we refer to in poetry and song resides, I suspect, in our mind. We often separate the two. People will say, ***"I followed my heart, not my mind."***

In my opening poem, at the beginning of Chapter 1, I say:

And though I'll always ponder
and pick and probe apart,
I've discovered that I'm different now;
the world is vast, but my world somehow
revolves not 'round my mind
but 'round my heart.

What that really means, of course, is that somewhere along the way I discovered it was wiser to go with my feelings rather than logical thought. Is that the same as doing what *feels* right as opposed to doing what we *know* is right? Can we separate the two? Can we, in fact, separate the mind from the soul or the soul from the heart? The more I ponder and pick apart, I find that it is all a part of the whole of who we are. We make decisions based on how we think *and* feel about a thing. We may sense that we are leaning in a particular direction based on our emotions rather than on what is more reasonable in any given circumstance, so we *think* we're leading with our *heart*. Some people insist that the true seat of our emotions is the heart, but is it? The heart pumps blood. Nobody has proven there even is a soul. Others believe it is our solar plexis, or the 3rd Chakra, which is the seat of our emotions and, therefore, the source of our personal power. As long as what we do rings true for us, does it really matter? Whether we make our choices by sleeping on it, praying over it, thinking about it, getting in touch with our gut feelings, or having our charkas aligned, the conclusion is ultimately the same.

For my purpose here, I'm speaking of the mind in at least two contexts: the thinking mind and the brain. The brain is the grey matter, the actual physical organ which controls the body and its functions. It is also the organ of the mind, through which the mind thinks. Each affects the other. Your mind can create better brain health by performing certain exercises. If the brain is damaged, it affects how the mind thinks and the subsequent behaviors displayed.

Leonardo da Vinci said: *"Men of lofty genius when they are doing the least work are most active."* I know it may not appear so to others, but when I seem idle, I am doing my best thinking, so I concur with da Vinci.

I think it was Einstein who said it, but I can't find the exact quote so I am paraphrasing: *".... we are all born geniuses. Some of us are just less damaged than others."*

Nourishing-the-Mind Processes

Come up with some brain exercises and mental challenges to keep your mind fresh, up and running. I have done a few things that gave me such a sense of accomplishment. I had long forgotten the capitals of all of the states, so I took the challenge and memorized the names of all the states alphabetically, and their capitals. It amazed me that I was still able to memorize such a long list. Geography was never my best subject, so I was determined to learn exactly where all the states were on the US map. I did that too. I have included a website which includes lots of fun ways to test yourself.

It is important to do this sort of thing on a regular basis. From time to time I go back and see how many state capitals I still remember, and if I can find all the states on the map in record time. If I don't do it for a while, some of it starts to go, so I do my best to exercise my brain regularly. Now, if I would only commit to exercising my body as often!

Before I leave this section, I want to make a distinction. Exercising the brain is not the same thing as challenging the mind, at least not in *my* mind. For me exercising the brain is memorizing things, taking quizzes, which are plentiful on the Internet. Challenging the mind, however, entails learning something new.

Some Suggestions to Exercise Your Brain:

1.   Find a blank map of the United States and see if you know where each state is.

       http://www.sheppardsoftware.com/web_games.htm

       That URL has online games and quizzes with the USA map and geography at different levels. See how much you remember, and if you need to, memorize the states and their capitals, and then try the quizzes again. If you do well, you can go to the next level, then the next and so on, each of which is increasingly more challenging. It is fun to see how much we can remember.

2.   Memorize the names of the presidents of the United States in the order in which they served, and then in alphabetical order.

Some Suggestions to Challenge your Mind:

1.   Learn a new language or a new software program on the computer.

2.   Learn a new piece of information every day and share it with someone to etch that new knowledge into your mind. One of the ways I do that is to pick a page randomly from one of my many non-fiction books. Two of my favorites for this endeavor are: **The BIG Book of TELL ME WHY** and its companion book **More BIG Book of TELL ME WHY**; both by Arkady Leokum.

They are filled with answers to hundreds of questions children ask. The questions are all-inclusive, covering such broad topics as our world, how things began, the human body, how other creatures live, and how things are made. Another book I love to learn fascinating facts from is **SEX LINK: The Three-Billion-Year-Old Urge and What the Animals Do About It,** by Hy Freedman. It is a classic. It reveals the sexual habits of insects and animals on land and sea.

Here is something I learned from that book: The female elephant, (of course), is pregnant for twenty-two months. You read that correctly, ladies. TWENTY-TWO months - the longest gestation period of any mammal. She has no interest in sex during that time or for the following three years, which makes an awful lot of sense, wouldn't you say? She spends those three years devoted to her calf.

Elephants go through a courtship more like humans than any other species. The sex act itself, however, is a little different. The male mounts the female's back, joins his genitals with hers, and then doesn't do much of anything else. The male's penis is motile; it thrusts and retreats on its own, sort of like a spring action. After all, 12,000 pounds of weight, even against another elephant, would be enough to knock her over. How wise is nature?

LAUGH OUT LOUD MOMENT

A Frenchman, an Englishman and a New Yorker were exploring the jungle and were captured by a fierce tribe. As they sit in a hut, awaiting their fate, the chief comes to them and says, "The bad news is we are going to kill you, and then use your skins to build a canoe. The good news is that you get to choose how you die."

114

The Frenchman says, "I take zee poison." The chief gives him poison. The Frenchman says, "Vive la France!" and drinks it down. He dies within seconds.

The Englishman says, "A pistol for me, please." The chief gives him a pistol, he points it at his head, says, "God save the queen!" and blows his brains out.

The New Yorker says, "Gimme a fork." The chief is puzzled, but he shrugs and gives him a fork. The New Yorker takes the fork and starts jabbing himself all over his stomach, his sides, his chest, everywhere he can reach. There's blood gushing all over the place. It's horrible. The chief is appalled and screams, "What are you doing?" The New Yorker looks at the chief and says, "So much for your canoe, dumb ass!"

As I grow older, I find I am
less concerned with my moving parts
and more with moving hearts.
I've learned the value of savoring each moment
as I would a tasty morsel.
There is no point in
swallowing your food whole;
it's like having sex when there is no love;
it may feed the body,
but it doesn't nourish the soul.

Nourishing the Spirit – minding the Soul

There is a difference, but to some, *spirit* and *soul* have become synonymous. It is my understanding and belief that the *spirit* of a person is their essence, and is rooted to their in-life personality. One's spirit depicts the sacred energy of the soul as it expresses on the earth plane. The *soul* exists with you throughout your many incarnations and is that which transcends the body.

My purpose here, however, is not to discuss or persuade you about other-worldly things. My aim is to guide you to a place where your soul can rest and your spirit can soar as you learn to be fully who you are right here, right now.

Toward that goal, I may interchange spirit and soul.

Our souls cannot rest if we harbor a grudge toward anyone, yet sometimes we hang on to the need to be right even if it creates a life-long wedge between us and someone we love or once loved. We just cannot seem to let it go. So many people feel wronged and are so sure they are right that they don't even try to understand the other person's point of view.

Resentment is like taking poison and waiting for the other person to die.
- Malachy McCourt -

In order to best nourish our spirit, our soul, healthy relationships are vital. It is a wise practice to consciously strive to keep them healthy, and cultivate them. However, it is, perhaps, as important, to know when to let a relationship go. When making amends is no longer viable, or we have forgiven, but cannot forget a transgression or hurt, sometimes we need to pull away for a while or altogether. We can wish each other well, be grateful for the good there was, the lessons learned and move on without regret or resentment. And it is not only OK to cry over the loss, I would recommend it. In fact, I encourage having a good cry every now and then. It is a release and very emotionally cleansing. Perhaps you are familiar with the 1987 movie, "Broadcast News" with Holly Hunter, Albert Brooks and William Hurt. Hunter plays the character Jane Craig, an uber-intense, very effective TV news producer who ritualistically cries every morning at her desk before she starts her day. The first time we see her crying we assume something terrible has happened, but we soon learn it is a daily routine. She allows herself a one to two minute good, sobbing cry and then shakes it off, wipes her eyes and goes on with her day.

I cannot leave the subject of "crying" without stressing how important it is to allow ourselves to cry from time to time, to grieve over losses or when significant changes occur in our lives. We read books and hear lectures about moving through the hard times, keeping a stiff upper lip, and all that, and while it is all well and good to keep a positive outlook, and to see problems as challenges, we are, after all, still human, as divine as we also are, and we must not lose sight of that. A good cry can do wonders to lift our spirits, as long as we see it for what it is and move on. *We are not admitting defeat when we momentarily feel defeated.* Just as we may make mistakes, but we are not a mistake. It is not healthy to push down sad or what we have termed negative emotions all the time; we can clog up our nervous and emotional systems. We put ourselves in real danger of a true breakdown down the line should that dam finally break.

Relationship to self, to God or whatever Higher Power to which you may subscribe, to family, to one significant other, to friends, to neighbors, to coworkers, to people you merely rub shoulders with in the course of a day, in the span of a life – all potentially nourish the soul or deplete it.

More of us, more than we might at first suspect, are living custom-made rather than off-the-rack lives. We may not be consciously aware of the design we have created for our lives, we may not like what we have made, but the gift is that we can always create a new design. If your life is not working for you, if your relationship *to* life and to others is less than you desire, commit to making some changes. You will better serve yourself and those around you by refusing to settle for an off-the-rack life because resentment is toxic to all involved. Remember, if you mistake **what is** for reality, it **becomes** your reality. The good news is that if you choose to, you can envision beyond what you see with your physical eyes, and create what it is you truly desire. Your new vision can become your new reality.

You must decide which is more important to you: being right or being kind, standing your ground or being understanding.

I can hear some of you thinking, ***"But sometimes I have to stand my ground."*** I would never suggest anyone be a doormat in any relationship. I am not asking you to put yourself in your pocket and for the sake of peace, give in or give up when an issue is important to you. The gift is in knowing when to compromise. It is one of the most important building blocks of character and a vital component in creating healthy relationships. There is nothing wrong with compromise. It is an essential ingredient in most human relationships. The distinction, however, must be made between compromising and ***being compromised***. I alluded to it in another chapter. Many people confuse the two. They believe all and any compromise is tantamount to ***being*** compromised. That is simply not true.

When you feel impelled to compromise, you need to ask yourself a few questions:
1. Are you compromising just to please someone else?
2. Are you compromising in order not to rock the boat?
3. Are you compromising in an effort to move to a more peaceful place where understanding is more important than being right?
4. Are you compromising or are you being compromised?
5. Will you be out of integrity if you compromise in this situation?

While in college, I wrote this little poem:

Let me not be tolerant so much as accepting,
for tolerance implies an ulterior superiority at best,
while acceptance implies an open reception to
the differences of others.

We all have strong opinions, but issues becoming non-issues revolves around degree and intensity and, perhaps, even more strongly on **intention**. Compromising is not relinquishing your principles. Compromising is coming to a place of common ground in an attempt to create a win-win situation. Of course, some people are intent on making an issue out of everything. The term **extenuating circumstances** does not ring an internal bell for them. Their slogan might be: ***It's my way or the highway***; their mantra: **UNMOVING, I AM A STONE. IN MOVING, I CRUMBLE**. There is no give, no compromise in those who fear they will break if they bend even a little. Perhaps, then, the true measure of a person is not where they stand, but under what circumstances they are willing to bend.

Does that mean we should *never* take a stand? Of course not. Having the courage of our convictions is something towards which most of us strive. Having convictions is a noble thing, and I don't think we should compromise our principles in times of challenge and controversy, or ever compromise who we inherently are. Certainly not for gain, neither just to please another, nor in order to fit in, or to go along with the crowd. I wish this could be brought home, especially, to young people today.

However, while having the courage of our convictions is essential to our character, being so sure that our take on things is ***the*** truth in any given situation, therefore, summarily dismissing the opinions of others, invites a life of constant turmoil. Being open to the differences of others allows you to expand your vision, stretch your boundaries and live more at peace with those around you. It also provides an opportunity for you to learn and grow. Compromising in certain situations, bending a little to please someone when the matter is clearly so much more important to them than your particular belief or preference in that moment is to you, can be a loving thing to do.

Often, in order to prevent the escalation of violence, compromise is the wise thing to do.

118

Is asking for advice compromising yourself? Have you ever gone to someone and said, *"I need your advice."* – and then after they have given it, gone on to someone else to ask their advice? The truth is that very few of us genuinely ask for advice. Rather, we seek those whose opinions are aligned with our own most deeply held, then shout, *"Aha! That's the answer! That's what I've been waiting to hear!"*

For some of us, seeking advice is an admission that we are compromising ourselves by giving up our own decision-making power. Of course it isn't anything of the kind. We compromise ourselves when we close ourselves off from the many possible alternative solutions to any given problem or challenge.

Of course there are those to whom we go for advice who tend to think we have asked for hard and fast directions or orders, for when we don't take their advice, they are hurt and or angry.

Compromise is an interesting concept. Some people are prepared to compromise at work, but not in their personal relationships. They view the former as wise and strategic, the latter, as weak and submissive. The opposite is true of other people; they are prepared to compromise at home, but not in a professional environment. They may view the former as wise, loving and strategic, the latter, as weak and ineffective.

Some of us may claim we don't care what others think, but I believe most of us really do; and that it is just the degree to which we care that differs. Those who care too deeply or solely about what others think rather than about what they think, are walking on quicksand. They will soon lose themselves in the quagmire. Those who don't care at all, or, who, at least, go about the business of their lives pretending they don't care what others think, will soon find themselves alone, or surrounded by inauthentic people who yes them to death.

No one person can have things their way 100% of the time. Anyone who believes they can or should is a tyrant, a bully or a fool. Any person who gives in all the time at work or at home is not compromising, they *are **being** compromised*. They are in a no-win-no-how-no-time scenario. Neither extreme is healthy.

Compromising, at its best, can create nothing short of a win-win scenario, in which both or all parties have their needs met, perhaps not in the way they would most prefer, but in a way that is agreeable, a way they can live with peacefully, and even happily. As the words to that old song, "The Glory of Love" tell us...." *"you've got to give a little, take a little..."*

Ready for a humorous aside? Isn't it fascinating how difficult it is for some of us to compromise with the human species, yet for our pets, no compromise, no sacrifice is too great? Well, here is an anonymous rant, allegedly posted very low on a refrigerator door:

Dear Dogs and Cats:

The dishes with the paw prints are yours and contain your food. The other dishes are mine and contain my food. Placing a paw print in the middle of my plate and food does not stake a claim for it becoming your food and dish, nor do I find that aesthetically pleasing in the slightest.

The stairway was not designed by NASCAR and is not a racetrack. Racing me to the bottom is not the object. Tripping me doesn't help because I fall faster than you can run.

I cannot buy anything bigger than a king sized bed. I am very sorry about this. Do not think I will continue sleeping on the couch to ensure your comfort. Dogs and cats can actually curl up in a ball when they sleep. It is not necessary to sleep perpendicular to each other, stretched out to the fullest extent possible. I also know that sticking tails straight out and having tongues hanging out on the other end to maximize space is nothing but sarcasm.

For the last time, there is no secret exit from the bathroom! If, by some miracle, I beat you there and manage to get the door shut, it is not necessary to claw, whine, meow, and try to turn the knob or get your paw under the edge in an attempt to open the door. I must exit through the same door I entered. Also, I have been using the bathroom for years - canine/feline attendance is not required.

The proper order for kissing is: Kiss me first, and then go smell the other dog or cat's butt. I cannot stress this enough...

One more thing, staring at me while I eat to try to direct my mind to give you my food will not work (usually). I am too old and too tired. Go stare at the kids. They are younger and more susceptible to mind control. If you don't believe me, notice how they all dress alike so they can be individuals.

Finally, in fairness, dear pets, I have posted the following message on the front door:

TO ALL NON-PET OWNERS WHO VISIT AND LIKE TO COMPLAIN ABOUT OUR PETS:

(1) They live here. You don't.

(2) If you don't want their hair on your clothes, stay off the furniture. That's why they call it 'fur'-niture.

(3) I like my pets a lot better than I like most people.

(4) To you, they are animals. To me, they are adopted sons/daughters who are short, hairy, walk on all fours and don't speak clearly.

Remember, dogs and cats are better than kids because they:
(1) Eat less

(2) Don't ask for money all the time

(3) Are easier to train

(4) Normally come when called

(5) Never ask to drive the car

(6) Don't hang out with drug-using people

(7) Don't smoke or drink

(8) Don't want to wear your clothes

(9) Don't have to buy the latest fashions

(10) Don't need a gazillion dollars for college, and

(11) If they get pregnant, you can sell their children

NOURISHING-THE-SOUL PROCESSES:

1. **JOURNAL!** If you haven't already started journaling, as suggested in an earlier chapter, begin now. Write down how you feel, what you think, why you reacted a certain way, your impressions about life, what you hope for, dream about, and desire above all else. (To truly *Journal Power Up Your Life*, check out http://www.createwritenow.com/ with Mari L. McCarthy for some wonderfully guided journaling challenges.)

2. **TRUST IN YOURSELF!** Listen to that still, small voice within. Once you become aware of your inner stirrings, your intuition will develop and your instincts will be spot on. Life will become easier, richer.

3. **TAKE TIME FOR YOU!** Make time every day to do something just for you.

4. **SNAP OUT OF IT!** (I love that line from the movie "Moonstruck." Rent it. It will make you howl. It will make you think. Two of my favorite things to do.)

OK, so perhaps you're depressed and "snapping out of it" doesn't seem a ready solution.

Did you know that depression has been described as anger turned inward? When we are depressed, we often punish ourselves by not doing things that bring us joy. Depression may be our way of stepping off life's treadmill for a while because we are so damned mad at ourselves for the wrong thinking which created bad choices, which resulted in a *less-than* life. Less than we planned, less than we thought we deserved. Well, it's time to **SNAP OUT OF IT!** You have suffered long enough. Let yourself off the hook. Tie a knot at the end of that short supply of rope, and swing on it! Start looking for reasons to smile, for things to do that bring you joy, for the kind of people who challenge you, cheer you, encourage you, make you laugh, make you think, and, perhaps, most important of all, who *make you feel good about yourself.*

Years ago, when I was in college, a friend asked if I'd had fun on my date the night before. I smiled and said, "Of course, I did. *I* was there." On the surface, that may sound brash or conceited, but the unabashed truth is that I can usually bring enough to any situation to find it or make it interesting or, at least, amusing.   Cultivate that in yourself. Remember what I said earlier, the only people who are ever truly bored are probably boring people. There is so much in life to learn, to see, to do, to experience, to appreciate.   You can cut out of life as big a slice as you want. You can only be bored if you throw away the scissors to your imagination.

5. **BE GRATEFUL!** Back to that again, I know. And I know, too, that it is hard to be grateful when life does not feel good. That is the time, though, that we most need to be grateful, if only for the experience of being alive to still learn some lessons. To best do that, you may need to come to terms with your notion of God or, at the very least, your concept of the meaning of life. Can you have a happy life if you do not believe in God? I think many people do. However, I believe that most truly happy people practice having an attitude of gratitude whether they give thanks to God, the Universe or life itself.

If you grapple with the idea of God and it is important to you, find someone you can talk to about your faith or lack thereof. It might be a member of the clergy or just a wise friend.

You may prefer to go to the library. In the Internet Age, where information is literally at our fingertips in vast quantities, I suspect libraries are less crowded these days. Nonetheless, go to the library or a book store and browse the shelves, heavy with inspirational books that address the big questions like: Why am I here? What is my purpose? Where is the nearest Pizza Hut? (Sorry. It must be time for lunch!)

Run your fingers along the spines of the books, open up the ones that call to you. Check out the table of contents, read a few pages and choose the one that feels right. Then read it and make notes in a composition book about those things you want to explore further.

6. **FORGIVE!** Forgiving is perhaps the quickest way to nourish our soul. We have all been told that forgiving is more for the person who does the forgiving than for the person forgiven. It may not feel like that when we have been holding on to that ***unforgiveness*** so long we have convinced ourselves that on some psychic level we have thwarted the ultimate happiness of the other person simply by clinging to the grudge or resentment.

7. **LOOK FOR THE GIFT!** There is a story about two young boys about to celebrate their eighth birthday. They were each individually brought into a room filled with horse manure, and told they would find their present inside. The first boy entered the room, and his nostrils were assaulted by the odor. He ran out of the room, screaming how unfair it was that he had been given a room full of dung for his birthday. The second boy was brought into the same room. He took a whiff, saw the dung and shouted gleefully: ***"Hand me a shovel. With all this horse manure around, there must be a pony in here somewhere!"***

8. LOOK AT THE BRIGHT SIDE! There is a bumper sticker that reads: **NO ONE EVER HURT THEIR EYES BY LOOKING AT THE BRIGHT SIDE OF THINGS.** Nice way to go through life, don't you think? I know that my sense of humor has been my saving grace. It not only helps me to look at the bright side of things, it lets me see life at an angle so that I don't mistake the light at the end of the tunnel for a train that is coming full speed right at me.

9. CULTIVATE A SENSE OF HUMOR! Even in the most difficult situations, I try to find something amusing. It can be uplifting, even refreshing, to remain cheerful amidst the rubble, although it can also be disconcerting to others at funerals, I must admit. My brother was always joking or fooling around at funerals when we were kids. I realize now, of course, that laughing was his defense mechanism when he was nervous or scared. Nonetheless, I will hang on to the laughter. I think it is the highest form of emotional intelligence. I know it has kept me from going crazy, well, at least, from going completely crazy.

I was not allowed to date all through high school, but once I started college I was not only expected to date, I was encouraged to date, to find a guy, get married, and have babies. And in that very order, thank you very much. Well, when I was twenty-four, I did become engaged, but called it off a month before the wedding. For a while my mother held prayer groups; in fact, I think she had my ten aunts doing round the clock novenas. At yet another cousin's wedding, my Aunt Rose came up to me, and, once again, pointed at the bride, poked me in the ribs and said, ***"You never know...you could be next!"*** She finally stopped doing that after, at the next funeral, I pointed to the corpse, gently poked my Aunt Rose in the ribs, and said softly, ***"You never know, you could be next."***

I have been in a wonderful uncommon law marriage for almost twenty years. I have had no biological children; at least not in this lifetime. I have been told by several psychics that I had fourteen children in a previous life. It must be true; I still have the stretch marks to prove it! The truth is I don't mind growing older—it is the growing wider that I mind. A mind may be a terrible thing to waste, but, I have to tell you, a waist is a terrible thing to mind.

Aging is a funny thing, if we keep our sense of humor about it. I remember when "getting lucky" meant dinner out and a night of romance. Now it means I had a good bowel movement! Another bumper sticker I love reads: **I FINALLY GOT MY SHIT TOGETHER AND MY BODY FELL APART.** It is some comfort, though, to know that gravity is no respecter of gender.

When I was the training officer in a large multi-branch bank in South Florida years ago, I attended a train-the-trainer weekend seminar in Jacksonville. There were a variety of workshops throughout the weekend, but the most infamous turned out to be the one in which we were instructed how to dress for success in the banking world.

About twenty of us sat in chairs in a circle around the workshop leader, who had long since taken his jacket off to be more comfortable. He started with the men. He said that bankers need to present themselves in a way that engenders trust, so the men were never to wear loud colors or pattern shirts, and absolutely never to wear plaid anything because it would make them look like shifty used-car salesmen, he said. They were, in fact, told to wear dark brown or navy blue suits with shoes to match, no loud ties, no gaudy jewelry and no heavy cologne.

Then he turned to the women. He said even though we worked in Florida, woman should never wear open-toe shoes, must always wear stockings, (or pantyhose), no strong perfume, no gaudy jewelry, preferably skirts over pant suits, and then he paused before his big finish, "...and women must never go bra-less to work because it is unseemly and distracting."

Some of the men laughed; some of the women blushed. I raised my hand. "Yes," he responded. I said, "I don't think that's fair. I mean I would never go to work bra-less because being a double D, I'd be tripping over myself all day." (Pause for laughter.) "But some women certainly could go without a bra. Still, perhaps it is prudent to wear one to work, but if women have to be held to that kind of standard, then the men should have to wear jockey briefs as opposed to boxer shorts." The men laughed again. Oddly, the leader unconsciously pulled up his pants..

I was just getting started. "For instance, there is an officer at my branch, an older gentleman, who wears boxers and it is very distracting when he sits in meetings with his legs spread far apart." (More laughter.) I continued. "You can see very clearly the outline of his male paraphernalia and that he wears it on the left. It is embarrassing and very distracting."

The leader said, "That's ridiculous. You can't tell if a man is wearing boxer shorts or jockey briefs." I said, "Yes, I can and I can tell you what side they wear it on." Again, he pulled up his pants, making it very obvious to me that he wore boxers and he wore his paraphernalia on the right and I told him so. Now it was his turn to blush.

"That was just a fluke," he said. Then he asked eight of the men to place their chairs in a semi circle within the larger circle and to have a sit. The leader said, "Go ahead. I dare you to tell me who's wearing jockies and who's wearing boxers."

125

I stood up, went right down the line, calling out, "Jockey, Jockey, boxer right, jockey, boxer left, boxer left, jockey, boxer right." The women were hysterical. Some of the men laughed, others closed their legs.

They gave me the nickname "Jockey" and called me that for the rest of the weekend.

Nonetheless, life is good at any age as long as you are open to the changes. I am well past post menopausal, but I still look forward to new adventures. Who would have guessed that at my age I would be into S & M! Yeah, that's right, S & M - **S**enior Discounts and **M**etamucil! Had you going there for a minute, didn't I?

10. **DO CREATIVE THINGS!** Some of us know we are creative; others are convinced they are not. The truth is we are all creative….just in different ways. You don't have to be a painter, a sculptor, a dancer, or a writer to be creative, but for some people just saying they are creative would be akin to accepting the burden of producing a work of art. Doing creative things versus *being creative* lifts that burden.

Being creative or inventive can be expressed by cooking, taking things apart and fixing them, or making a scrapbook. Whether or not you believe you are creative, you can enlist the activity of *doing creative things* to further nourish your soul.

Some suggestions for being Creative:

- o **Paint by number** – it may seem childish, but there are some truly beautiful paintings available to do "by the number" and it might unleash a desire in you to paint something on your own.

- o **Read and memorize poetry** – it can be fun to memorize poetry and then recite a particular one when it seems appropriate. You may find yourself writing a verse now and then.

- o **Put together jig-jaw puzzles** of landscapes, seascapes or animals and frame them to hang in your home or give as gifts.

- o **Sew something** for yourself or a loved one. Buy a simple pattern and make something, even if it's just a bib for a friend's new baby, or matching aprons for a newly married couple. It can be both creative and challenging.

126

o **Write in a daily journal**.

o **Write the story of your life**. Put together a timeline of your life, listing all the major events that have helped shape your personality. There is a wonderful book called: Every Person's Life is Worth a Novel by Erving Polster. Check it out. You might want to use it as a guide to create your story; a fine legacy to leave for your family.

o **Visualize**. Use your fertile imagination to visualize your life as you would like it to be. Take a specific area in which you would like to see some changes, close your eyes and go for it. See yourself doing and being in the world as the person you want to be, or, rather, as the person you truly are. Make a **TREASURE MAP BOARD** to accompany it.

o **LISTEN TO MUSIC** – Not just your favorite; broaden the experience by listening to music you might not ordinarily. If you usually listen to Classical music, try Country or Jazz. If you usually listen to Soft Rock or Hard Rock, try Classical.

o **LEARN TO PLAY AN INSTRUMENT**. Even if you just learn to play a few basic chords on the guitar or piano, you can enjoy making music!

o **Dare to do things differently** even if the world at large thinks you are nuts.

I love this ad for "geniuses" from Apple:

"Here's to the crazy ones. The misfits. The rebels. The trouble-makers. The round pegs in the square holes. The ones who see things differently. They're not fond of rules, and they have no respect for the status-quo. You can quote them, disagree with them, glorify, or vilify them. But the only thing you can't do is ignore them. Because they change things. They push the human race forward. And while some may see them as the crazy ones, we see genius. Because the people who are crazy enough to think they can change the world, are the ones who do."

11. **CHOOSE TO BE JOYFUL**. Many of us were raised in families where there seemed to be little joy. Instead, there were cautionary tales of *"You can't expect to be happy all the time, you know…."* - *"Life is hard…get used to it…."* – *"You think life is just one big joke, don't you?"* - *"You're born, you suffer, you die…"*

Is our capacity for joy learned or is there a gene we inherit which determines our capacity for joy? I think the jury is still out on that one, but I know we can cultivate it on our own simply by *choosing* to be joyful. Again, let us not confuse *simple* with *easy*.

Nonetheless, one of the quickest ways to do that is by choosing the company we keep. I read the following quote somewhere years ago and it stuck with me. Sadly, I cannot remember who wrote it and cannot give it proper credit, but I have to share it with you: *"Without doubt, the most common weakness of all human beings is the habit of leaving their minds open to the negative influence of other people."* A friend's mother wrote in my sixth grade graduation book: *"Sometimes in order to make your life add up, you must subtract some people from it."* Who do you spend most of your time with?

Choosing, of course, is about deciding. Life is not all about what has happened to you; much of it is about what you have allowed and, perhaps, even summoned by your most consistent words and thoughts. Why not choose joyful thoughts, joyful words and joyful companions?

12. **SPEND TIME**. Do you waste time, kill it, or spend it wisely? I have never been flattered when an invitation to spend time with someone was broached with, *"Want to kill a few hours?"* I understand there are some husbands who consider it foreplay to tell their wives, *"Let's go upstairs and kill a few minutes."* We have all wasted time or, at least, felt we have. The older I get, the more I wonder if there *is* such a thing as wasted time because it all seems to matter in the big scheme of things. As with most things, it is all in our frame of reference. Do you consider it a waste of time to do chores? I know I have, especially if there was something else I wanted to do instead, but in retrospect I can see that doing chores is not a waste of time, it is just a different way of spending it. According to Henry David Thoreau:

"Time is a cruel thief to rob us of our former selves. We lose as much to life as we do to death. Take time to deliberate; but when the time for action arrives, stop thinking and go in. All my possessions for a moment of time. As if you could kill time without injuring eternity. "

128

It has been said that when we are doing something we love, the time does not seem long enough, but when we are doing something we do not want to do, time seems to drag on forever. If you are doing something wonderful, savor it. If you are doing something you do not enjoy or do not want to do, but feel you must do, or there is an unpleasant aspect of your job, know this: You don't have to love everything you do, but you can choose to do everything you do **with love**. It makes all the difference.

13. **GIVE YOURELF THE GIFT OF TIME.** Do not beat yourself up if you haven't met a certain timetable of where you thought you would be by a certain age, and do not dare think that idle time is wasted time. Time spent daydreaming is a form of visualization. Most of the great inventors have had their revelations, their epiphanies when they were not working diligently, but when they were taking a break or doing a task unrelated to their major task.

> "Everything has a gestation period, a time period that must pass before things will come into form. If you plant a carrot seed, it takes about seven weeks for the sprout to make its above-dirt entrance. Bamboo, which can grow up to thirteen feet in as little as one week, takes up to seven years to break through the surface of the ground. But for seven long years it looks like absolutely nothing's happening. Now that takes some commitment." - James Arthur Ray from **Harmonic Wealth**

"Life is not measured by the number of breaths we take, but by the moments that take our breath away." - Hilary Cooper

14. **HAVE SOMETHING TO CARE ABOUT AND CARE *FOR*.** If you do not already have one, consider adopting a pet. We all want someone or some *thing* to care about, but what we may *need* even more is someone or some thing to care *for*. A pet gives you a kind of unconditional love that is impossible to duplicate. I firmly believe that if our significant others greeted us at the door panting, wagging their imaginary tails, and jumping with joy at the sight of us, countless marriages would be in a lot better shape! If a pet is out of the question for some reason, plant a flower or vegetable garden you can tend to, or buy indoor plants, an herb globe, something that needs your attention.

15. **HAVE FAITH.** If not in a higher power, have faith in yourself and in the process of life. Some people say: "Life sucks!" I say: *Sometimes it may appear that life sucks, but think of is as a friendly tug from the Universe meant to keep you grounded!* Suffering

129

happens to us for one or all of these reasons: (1) to instruct us, (2) to purify us, (3) to motivate us, (4) to test our resolve or faith. I believe we go through emotional crap for the same reason literal crap goes through us - to cleanse and detoxify us. I also fervently believe that no matter how down and out you may sometimes feel, especially if you are out of work and temporarily out of money, you must not allow yourself to feel *spiritually* bankrupt. You can tie that knot on the proverbial rope and hang on to the knowledge that you own your emotional intelligence, your sense of humor, your passion for life...and you are filled with a great capacity for joy. Be your own best comforter, let your internal cheer leader remind you every day that you are stronger than any circumstance or difficulty, and that better times are coming.

Chapter 17

THE RIGHT WORDS AT THE RIGHT TIME

I loved my mother's singing voice;
I loved certain dishes that she cooked;
I loved her genuinely sweet disposition,
and when she read my poetry...
I just loved the way she looked.
A smile, sometimes a tear or two,
told me more than words of praise.

Once, when I was upset, she told me
she didn't know what to say.
So, I told her in a poem,
hoping she would understand,
that I felt comforted by her touch alone.
Now years later, my mother is gone,
and I am comforted still,
for when I look down at my own,
I see my mother's hands.

Once, when I was thirteen years old and was angry with my mother, I told her I loved her but that I did not like her. I regretted those words the veritable moment that I said them, but they were out there in the cosmos, and they cut deeply into my mother's heart. It took many more words and not just a few years before I was able to convince her that those words were said in anger and I did not mean them.

Words are powerful things. They can hurt or comfort, discourage or encourage, insult or compliment, condemn or praise, crush or lift someone's spirit.

Some years ago I discovered Marlo Thomas' book, <u>THE RIGHT WORDS AT THE RIGHT TIME</u>. It is a compilation of essays by various celebrities describing the impact on their lives of particular words said to them by certain people, or a phrase or saying that they heard in a film or read in a book that lingered and impacted their lives in a meaningful way. Some of the essays are more interesting than others, but it is worth a read. The concept alone stirred up some stuff for me.

It made me consider how crucial not only the right words are, but the right timing of those words. You have heard the expression ***"It can all turn on a dime."*** Our lives ***can*** turn on a dime; they can literally turn around 180 degrees in response to a single event: experiencing a loss, winning the lottery, stumbling upon your life partner, hearing a particular line in a movie, reading a certain phrase in a book, encountering a homeless person, meeting in person someone you have always admired.

Another familiar saying about the right timing is: ***"When the student is ready, the teacher appears."*** That is true enough, too. We can struggle and strain trying to learn something for months, maybe even years, seemingly in vain, and then we meet someone, or find a book which explains it so simply that we finally ***get*** it. What are we to take from that? Are we to give up the next struggle right away, placating ourselves that the timing is just off? I don't think so. I don't think giving up the struggle is the answer, but we might give up the suffering and straining over it, and know that if we persist, eventually we *will* GET IT, or will be led to something better or to a better way of accomplishing the same thing. My sister Rosemary has often counseled me prayerfully over the years with this saying: ***In God's time, not yours***. I have to tell you; sometimes I have wondered just what clock God uses. My mother always said, ***"Things have a way of working out in time."***

I have heard some ***right words*** from my mother, my father, favorite uncles and aunts, other family members and friends, and from teachers, especially Florence Crozier Hobbs, my second grade teacher, with whom I kept in touch until she passed. I have read some right ***words*** in countless books. I have already shared some throughout ***this*** book.

Here are more: From <u>The Four Agreements</u> by Miguel Ruiz:

1. Be impeccable with your word.

2. Don't take things personally.

3. Don't make assumptions.

4. Do the best you can.

For me, being impeccable with my word means saying what I truly mean. Ralph Waldo Emerson summed it up beautifully when he said: ***"What you do speaks so loudly that I cannot hear what you say."***

Not taking things personally is a real challenge, but one worth taking. It goes back to what Einstein said was the most important question to answer: Do we believe the Universe is *for* us or *against* us? People are not out to get us, and even when they say things we find hurtful or objectionable, we must consider the source of their pain, for it has to do with their own **stuff**, rather than us.

There is another popular saying: "Never **assume**; it makes an ass (**ass**ume) out of you (ass**u**me) and me (assu**me**)."

We are all in this together, doing the best we can, each of us struggling, learning, and growing. When we are mindful that everyone is truly doing the best they can, with their own level of knowledge, understanding and awareness, it gives us compassion for ourselves and others. Nobody wakes up in the morning with the intention of failing at life. Like the infant learning to walk, we are sometimes battered and bruised, but never defeated, not as long as we get back up each time, determined to do the best we can.

So, for all intents and purposes, life is not so much a matter of the conditions in our lives as much as it is about the consciousness which brought them into our experience, and the way we choose to respond to those conditions once confronted with them in **real** time.

Here are some parting words from me:

Perhaps it is all about mind over matter, or, rather, minding, as in **attending to**, what **really** matters. We can truly create a design for our lives. We are not at the mercy of the winds of fate or random events. Even if we have only a small part in creating the events of our lives, we certainly have the power to choose how we respond to what happens.

Another book with some **right words** for me at just the **right time** was first published in 1965. I read it in 1966 when I was nineteen. I was in the library at Hofstra University, looking for books related to a topic I was doing research on for a paper. Suddenly, a book flew off the shelf. I do not know how it was propelled, but I picked it up, read the title: **Advice from a Failure** (by Jo Coudert), and thought, ***"Uh…no, I don't think I need advice from a failure."*** I was about to return the book to the shelf when, instead, I decided to peruse the table of contents. It intrigued me. I sat down and began to read. It was the only book I borrowed from the library that day. I recently found a used copy of it on line, bought it and read it again. Some of the advice is a little off for the times we live in, but the part that spoke to me when I first read it, still spoke loudly to me.

I attended Hofstra on a full-tuition distinguished academic scholarship, and was under a great deal of pressure to maintain a certain grade point average, which had to go up each year in order to keep the scholarship. That, coupled with other familial stressors, had created the beginnings of a duodenal ulcer. I became so depressed, I even considered dropping out of school and running away from everyone who knew me. Then I found Codert's book and within its pages, there was a passage that hit home. Rather than paraphrase it, which I often do in workshops, I have taken it directly from the book:

"....if I fall downstairs and break my leg...whether I tripped or was pushed...it hurts (the same, no more) no less, and I am the only one who can see to the healing. I can take responsibility and do everything I can that is therapeutic, or I can point to someone else and say, 'You are why I shall limp the rest of my life.' There will be a certain satisfaction in pointing, but it will not alter the fact that I am the one who is crippled."

I had been pointing the finger of blame at a lot of things for all my problems. I blamed my depression on things that had happened to me as a child, on my caring but strict upbringing, on society, on the pressures of my scholarship....you name it. And there I was...an emotional cripple, afraid of so many things at a time in my life that should have been joyful and free. I chose right then and there to stop pointing the finger of blame and to take responsibility for my own happiness.

Does that mean I lived happily ever after, that I never blamed anyone else ever again for anything that ever happened in my life? Hardly! We are, after all, always works in progress, but, thanks to Jo Coudert's book, <u>Advice from a Failure</u>, and my continuing journey of self discovery, I was on my way and my path has been richer for it.

It is my humble wish that you will take something significant away with you from this book. Perhaps **my** words showed you something about yourself; maybe a funny personal story I shared made you laugh heartily about something in your life that had previously only brought you pain. Perhaps some processes you completed gave you a string of aha moments that created a needed shift in perspective. Perhaps you have applied some of the life strategies I suggested and you have been encouraged and inspired enough to look at life differently.

Whether you simply forge a better, more enriching experience of life, or step back from the edge if that is where you found yourself when you began reading this book, remember you can always tie a knot at the end of your rope and hang on. It is all in the timing, so please *give yourself all the time you need*.

Every time.

Smile and love yourself through it.

Breathe deeply. It is going to be all right.

I hope some of my words were the right words at the right time for you.

From my heart to yours, know this: there is a space in this world, in this life, only *you* can fill. Wake up and fill it to the brim and overflowing.

"This hole in my heart is in the shape of you.

No one else can fit it.

Why would I want them to?"

Jeanette Winterson

THE "RIGHT WORDS" PROCESSES

1) Was there ever a time when you said something to someone and regretted it almost immediately. Pick one of those times. Imagine you are with that person again, apologize for what you once said and tell them what you wished you had said, what you really meant to say. If that person is still around, you might want to say it to them in person.

2) Think of a time when you needed to hear some words of comfort, support and encouragement, but none came. In fact, what came were words of criticism, ridicule and discouragement. Now write down what you wanted to hear or wish you had heard as if it were coming from that very person, and express how hearing those words might have made a difference in your life at the time.

3) What were you told, what was said to you at some pivotal time in your life that made a difference for the better? Write down anything that comes to mind. If the person who gave you those encouraging words is still alive, visit them or call them and thank them. If they have passed, write them a letter giving thanks and send it off to the cosmos.

4) Have you said any encouraging words to anyone lately? Think about the significant people in your life and let them know what they mean to you, why you love and admire them.

5) Make it a habit to say uplifting things, even to strangers. Everyone is struggling with something. A kind word, even from a veritable stranger, can produce a significant shift in someone's consciousness. It can provide the sign looked for, the hope needed.

The next time you are in the supermarket, for instance, if the cashier looks tired or upset, find something you can say that would lift their spirits. Something like, "You're always so polite when I come to the store. Thank you." or "I saw you smile the other day. It becomes you." or "Congratulations! You showed a lot of patience with your last customer. Another cashier might have lost their cool."

I remember hearing the actor Ricardo Montalban once say that whenever he passed by a woman, he smiled at her. He added, "If they are pretty, it pleases me; if they are not, it pleases them." Sometimes no words are necessary. A nod acknowledging someone's presence, or a smile, can mean everything to someone who feels alone in the world.

It may just be that we are all angels on the earth with but one wing each, and that is why in order to fly...in order to soar, we must embrace one another.

APPENDIX

Camille's Comfort Food Recipes

One Last Process: Family Storybook

Acknowledgements

Bibliography

Suggested Reading

CAMILLE'S COMFORT FOOD RECIPES

This is my favorite photo of my mother, Josephine, and me. She passed in 1998.

Although she did not formally **teach** me how to cook, I learned a lot by just watching her. Mom was a good cook, but she did not particularly like to cook, so when I would experiment in the kitchen on weekends, Mom enjoyed the deserved break. I took on a few of her signature dishes, put in a twist to make them my own, and, of course, I created new concoctions too. She used to say she preferred my cooking because I flavored things differently, but I think food just tasted better to her when somebody else prepared it. In any case, thanks, Mom!

What is comfort food anyway, and why is it that so often after eating ***comfort food***, we feel so uncomfortable! Seriously, to me anything I enjoy cooking and eating is ***comfort food***, so that gave me a wide berth in choosing which of my favorite dishes to include here. It was a fun challenge, creating actual recipes out of them, because I seldom measure anything when I cook. I add things by eye, taste and experience. So, as I recreated each dish, I measured and wrote down how much I put in of each ingredient. Of course, we each have our own sense of taste, so feel free to use less or more salt,

138

pepper, garlic, etc., accordingly. Oh, and please never forget the most important ingredient: love. Too sappy for you? SNAP OUT OF IT! Because, although it may not be scientifically proven, food made by loving hands is healing, and, perhaps, the most delicious food in the entire world.

Enjoy! Mangiare! Buon appetito!

MENU

What Will be oN your MeNU toNight?

Spareribs, Lima Beans and Cabbage

Camille's Chicken Soup with Orzo

Sicilian Eyes (Eggs) with Tomatoes & Onions

Stuffed Artichokes

Slow Roasted Port Butt

Artichoke hearts, peas, onions and mushrooms

No-bake Piña Colada Pie

SPARERIBS, LIMA BEANS AND CABBAGE

Ingredients

1 large onion (diced)
2 garlic cloves (minced)
1 small can of tomato sauce
1 2-lb bag of large Lima beans
4 lbs of pork spareribs
(Have the butcher cut them into individual ribs for you!)
1 Tbsp of lemon juice
1 good sized head of cabbage (cut into slightly bigger than bite-sized wedges)
salt & pepper to taste
6 cups of water
1 qt of chicken broth or stock

Directions:

1.　　Prepare the Lima beans.
(I know the directions on the bag of Lima beans say to soak them overnight, but I just do the quick method of parboiling them for a few minutes, then take the pot off the heat and keep them in the water for over an hour.)
2.　　During that time, put the spareribs in a big bowl or pot with a few tablespoons of sea salt, and then cover them with cold water and 1 tablespoon of lemon juice. After a half hour, rinse off the spareribs under cold running water and put them in an 8-quart stock pot.
3.　　Drain the Lima beans and then put them in the pot with the spareribs.
4.　　Add the diced onions, minced garlic, water, chicken broth and can of tomato sauce.
5.　　Bring to a boil, and then add 3 tablespoons of salt and 1 teaspoon of pepper. (You can add more salt and pepper to taste later on.)
6.　　Lower the heat to medium-low and let the pork spareribs cook for at least two hours, so they are fall-off-the bone tender.
7.　　After at least two hours, add the cabbage, bring to a boil again, then lower to medium-low and let cook for 35 minutes or until tender.

I serve it with crusty bread and butter.

CAMILLE'S CHICKEN SOUP WITH ORZO

Ingredients

8 bone-in, skinless chicken thighs
2 Tbsp lemon juice
1 Tbsp table salt
2 Tbsp sea salt
1-2 cups of ORZO macaroni
1 small can of tomato sauce (optional)
2 medium onions (peeled and cut into quarters)
4 celery stalks (roughly chopped)
3 carrots (sliced at an angle or diced)
4 ears of corn (take husks off and any strands)
2 cloves of garlic (peeled and smashed)
8 cups of water
2 Tbsp "Better Than Bouillon" chicken base
1 quart box of Chicken Broth
Parmesan cheese (optional)

Directions:

1. Using kitchen shears, cut off any excess fat still left on chicken thighs.
2. Place thighs in a bowl, pour the sea salt over them; and then cover with cold water
3. Let them soak for a half hour, then drain and put thighs in 6 to 8-quart stock pot.
4. Add the water, lemon juice, tomato sauce, chicken base, carrots, onions and celery to the pot and bring to a boil.
5. Once it is boiling, lower heat to medium-low and add salt and pepper to taste and let it cook. for at least an hour and a half.
6. Take thighs out, cut the meat off the bone and put the chicken pieces back in the pot. Bring back up to a boil.
7. Break ears of corn in half and add to boiling soup and cook corn for ten minutes.
8. Add 1-2 cups of ORZO (use less if you like soupy soup), boil for 9-10 minutes, stirring the pot occasionally to prevent sticking to the bottom of the pot.
9. Serve with grated Parmesan cheese (optional).

SICILIAN EYES (EGGS) WITH TOMATOES & ONIONS

Ingredients

2 large eggs
2 slices of sour dough bread
2 Tbsps of butter
1 medium tomato (cut into wedges)
½ stick of butter
1 small onion (sliced)
1 tspn of orégano
1 tbspn of extra virgin olive oil (EVOO)

Directions for 2 Servings:

First make the Tomatoes & Onions:

1. Put ½ stick of butter in a 1-quart non-stick pot with the 1 tbsp of EVOO.
2. Add tomato wedges, onions, oregano, salt & pepper to taste.
3. Cook on medium heat, stir for a few minutes, then put heat on low to keep warm.

Sicilian Eyes:

1. Toast the sour dough bread. (medium)
2. Cut out a circle in the middle of each slice.
3. Heat non-stick pan to medium; add pieces of toast and circles to the pan.
4. Cut the 2 Tbsps of butter, placing some in each hole, and around the toast.
5. Add one egg to each hole.
6. Cover the pan, and cook to your liking. (Approximately 3 minutes gives you cooked white with soft yolk).
7. Serve with tomatoes and onions on the side or over the eggs.

STUFFED ARTICHOKES

First, realize that this is a labor-intensive recipe, but it is a labor of love, and, oh, so worth it!

Ingredients

2 Artichokes
(Choose ones that have no or only a few dark marks and whose leaves are opening a little at the top, and whose stems are firm.)
2 small lemons
1 Tbsp of Better than Bouillon Chicken base
Olive Oil
1 Tbsp of Garlic Powder
2 cups of Italian Seasoned or Panko Seasoned Bread Crumbs

Directions:

Note: Artichokes, once cut, will oxidize and turn black soon after hitting the air, so squeeze lemon juice on all cut edges as you go.

Preheat oven to 375 degrees F.

1. Mix the chicken base with the juice of one lemon, 2 Tbsps of olive oil and 2 cups of hot water. Add the garlic powder and then stir until the chicken base dissolves.
2. Pour half of liquid into a 9 x 13 glass pan.
3. Rinse the artichokes with cold water.
4. Using a very sharp, serrated knife, cut at least an inch off the tips of the artichokes, and cut only the bottom end of the stem off, as the stem can be eaten. Using scissors, cut off any remaining sharp points from the leaves. (Remember to squeeze lemon juice on all cut edges.)
5. Place 1 artichoke at a time onto cutting board, cut side down, and using that same sharp knife, cut the artichokes in half from the middle of the stem straight through. Peel the stems with a small, sharp knife, removing the hard outer layer.
6. Place the artichoke immediately into glass pan, cut side down in the liquid, and then do the same with the other choke.
7. Pour the remaining liquid over the artichokes.
8. Cover the glass dish with aluminum foil and seal it tight around all edges.
9. Place in preheated oven and let cook for at least an hour, depending on size of artichokes. If they are particularly large, let them cook an additional ten minutes.

10.   While the artichokes are cooking, make the stuffing:
11.   Put bread crumbs in a mixing bowl. Add enough olive oil to moisten the bread crumbs, add 1/2 a teaspoon of garlic powder if you are a fan, and then mix together.
12.   Heat non-stick frying pan on medium heat. Put bread crumb mixture into the pan, flatten with a wooden spoon, and let brown on the bottom for a couple of minutes. Be careful not to let it burn.
13.   Turn over the bread crumb mixture a portion at a time and brown the other side for another minute or so. Take off the heat, stir and let sit until artichokes come out of the oven.
14.   Once artichokes are out of the oven, (DO NOT TURN THE OVEN OFF!), carefully take off the aluminum foil and with tongs, remove the artichoke halves to a cutting board. Let cool a little bit. With a grapefruit spoon (which has sharp ridges), spoon out the fuzzy choke in the center of each half and discard. Empty liquid out of glass pan. Spray with olive oil cooking spray. Place the artichoke halves back in the pan.
15.   Spoon stuffing into each half and between the leaves, and then return the pan to the oven for twenty minutes.

Eat by pulling the leaves off and scraping with your bottom teeth the tender fleshy part of each leaf, scooping up some of the stuffing with each bite, adding salt to each leaf or dipping in your favorite dressing. The longer the artichoke cooks, the more tender parts you'll have to enjoy, but you don't want the bottom to get mushy, so don't overcook it. Just follow my time guidelines and you'll be fine.

Once all the leaves are off, enjoy the tender artichoke heart's bottom and stem.

(If the artichoke is big, as the California artichokes usually are, cook an additional 15 minutes; half an artichoke is enough for a single serving. If they are small to medium, you might consider serving both halves, or at least have extra halves on a separate dish on the table for those who would like a little more.)

SLOW ROASTED PORK BUTT

Ingredients

4-6 lb Pork Butt
1 large Lemon
2 cloves of Garlic - peeled and cut into 4 slices each -
2 large onions
1 Tbsp of Sea or Kosher Salt
1 tspn ground Cummin
1 tspn Garlic powder
1 tspn Onion powder
1/2 tspn of Paprika
1/2 tspn ground Pepper
Extra Virgin Olive Oil
NOTE: If you prefer, you can replace all items below the 2 large onions with a bottle of store-bought MOJO and marinate the pork butt in that overnight, adding the onions to the marinade.
Most of the liquid will be absorbed into the pork; you may put any remains in the roasting pan around the pork or discard.

Directions:

Preheat the oven to 425 degrees F. Dry off pork butt with paper towel.

1. There is usually a layer of fat on a pork butt. Do not cut it off! With a sharp knife, cut diagonal slices through that fatty layer side of the pork, and then from the other angle so that it looks like a diamond pattern. Make 8 small but deep cuts all around the pork and insert the garlic slices.
2. Squeeze juice of half the lemon over the pork, getting into the slits where the garlic is.
3. Drizzle 1 Tbsp of olive oil onto the pork, rub it all over the butt, then combine the sea salt, cummin, garlic powder, onion powder, paprika and pepper and rub onto all sides of the pork.
4. Place the pork into an aluminum-lined oven pan not much bigger than it is, but with room around the sides. (Spray the pan with olive oil cooking spray before and after you put the aluminum foil in it to keep the pork from sticking.)
5. Cook at that high temperature for 1 hour. Lower the temperature to 325 and let slow roast for 5 hours.

6. The last hour the pork is cooking, sauté that sliced large onion in some olive oil until it begins to carmelize. Place the sautéd onion around the pork so it picked up the flavor of the pork juices and squeeze the juice of the other half of the lemon over the pork. Let pork continue to cook for the last hour.

ARTICHOKES HEARTS, PEAS, ONIONS AND MUSHROOMS

Ingredients

2 packages of Bird's Eye frozen artichoke hearts
1 large package of fresh mushrooms (sliced)
1 package of frozen sweet peas (defrosted)
1 large onion (sliced)
1 Tbsp of oregano
salt and pepper
garlic powder
extra virgin olive oil
butter

Directions:

1. Cook artichoke hearts according to package directions. (I do them in the microwave.)
2. Sauté sliced onion and mushrooms in 1 tablespoon each of olive oil and butter in medium sized pot.
3. Add the cooked artichoke hearts and the defrosted package of peas.
4. Add salt, pepper, and garlic powder to taste, and the 1 tablespoon of oregano.
5. Stir occasionally, and cook over medium heat for twenty minutes.
6. Pour 2 more tablespoons of extra virgin olive oil over the vegetables just before serving.

NO-BAKE Piña Colada Pie *

Ingredients

3/4 cup pineapple-coconut nectar
1 cup light coconut milk (Shake can well before opening.)
1 teaspoon rum extract
1 (3.4-ounce) box of **instant** vanilla pudding and pie filling
1 cup shredded coconut meat
8 ounces whipped topping, divided (Cool Whip)
1 (9-inch) pre-baked pie crust or a Ready Graham Cracker Crust (plain or chocolate)

Directions:

1. In a large bowl, combine nectar, coconut milk, and 1 teaspoon rum extract.
2. Sprinkle pudding mix over liquid and whisk for 2 minutes.
3. Fold in coconut and 1/2 of the whipped topping.
4. Pour into pre-baked pie crust and chill in refrigerator for 2 to 3 hours.
5. Just before serving, spread remaining whipped topping over top of pie.

*This is a simple and delicious recipe. I've been making it a long time and can't remember where I found the recipe, so I cannot give proper credit.

<u>One last Process: Family Storybook</u>
Make a scrapbook story book of your family.
Here are some examples of mine:

Picture it: Brooklyn - 1947

A small gathering of family & friends for my brother's fifth birthday! That's my father, Johnny behind my brother Johnny, & Mom (Josie), holding four-month old me. My paternal grandmother, Carmela, is first on your left. My maternal grandmother, Rosalia, is behind my father, with my maternal grandfather, Salavatore, to her right (your left). My maternal Aunt Mary is in front of him, holding my favorite cousin Rosalie. Between Dad and his mother, at the corner of the table, is my Dad's youngest brother; that's right, my Uncle Joey, who is about the same age as my brother. My cousin Marie, Rosalie's sister, is standing over me and her brother Joey is at the table next to me. To your far right is my father's brother Tony. Next to my Uncle Tony is Rose, a friend of the family, with her mother next to her and her husband behind her. Her son is sitting next to my cousin Joey. (Are you getting all this?) Next to Rose's husband is my cousin Nicky.

150

Nicky was Aunt Mary's only child. His father, my Uncle Sal, is in the back row, peeking through. My maternal Aunt Rosie (mother of Marie, Joey and Rosalie) is standing in the back on your left. The other woman, baby and girl standing between my Grandma Rosalia and Uncle Sal are people I don't remember.

Grandma Rosie (Mom's mother) and Grandma Carmela (Dad's mother) married in Sicily when they were just fourteen years old. Can you imagine? My paternal grandmother had twelve children. Two died in childhood. The ten remaining consisted of six girls and four boys. My father was the oldest. My maternal grandmother had fourteen children; eleven died in childhood. My mother and her two sisters, Mary and Rose, were the only survivors. My mother was the youngest and the third to be named Josephine.

July 1961: My mother Josephine is on your right, her sister, my Aunt Rosie, is in the middle and her sister, my Aunt Mary, is on the left. They were very close. Mom used to say, "We're small, medium and large." Mom and Aunt Mary sang; Mom was an alto, Aunt Mary was a soprano. She sang on the radio for a time. Mom also played piano by ear. Aunt Rosie was not a singer, although we enjoyed when she sang "The 50 cent song." She was married to the leader of the band, Uncle Joe.

That's the smiling duo of my brother Johnny & me with me in the middle and me again, at three years old. I was "flower girl" at my cousin Nicky's wedding.

I wore lipstick that day, but wasn't allowed to wear makeup again until I was 16.

That's my sister Rosemary (3 years younger) and doll friend on the left, and on your right you see my cousin Rosalie and me. I saw Rosalie at least once a week growing up. She always said I was her lawyer because I would talk to her father in her defense whenever she was in trouble, which wasn't really very often. Between the food, the music and getting to spend time with my cousin, I have a lot of happy memories from Aunt Rosie's house.

That's me on your left, my sister Rosemary squatting on the piano, and brother Johnny at the piano in our apartment in Brooklyn, New York in 1952. Johnny grew up to play lead and bass guitar, as well as sing. My sister toyed with the banjo, guitar and drums at different times. I took to the piano, but was not serious enough to take lessons from Uncle Joe, so I taught myself to play with FAKE books. I tried my hand at the guitar in my early twenties, but did not like the calluses it produced, so I stayed with the piano. When I moved out on my own at 24, the first thing I bought was my Kohler & Campbell piano. I still have it at this writing, 42 years later.

My brother Johnny

Sadly, my beloved brother lost his battle with brain cancer at 69, passing in December of 2011. I miss him terribly.

153

This is my favorite photo of Mom. Uncle Joe took the photograph. I guess it was her **glamour** shot. Mom had a beautiful voice. It was rich, sweet and pure. As long as there was music, she was happy, and when she was singing, she was the best of who she was. Her signature song was "Anema E Core" (With All My Heart and Soul). She battled cancer for two years, passing in October of 1998.

Uncle Joe, "the leader of the band," taught most of us to play some instrument or other. He played banjo, guitar and mandolin. That's his wife, Aunt Rosie, with him. She played piano as well as accordion.

Uncle Joe loved music. He played with such passion, leaning into the guitar or banjo. He had a big, booming voice and when he was giving private lessons on whatever instrument, he sometimes raised his voice which sounded like he was angry, but he wasn't' he just took it very seriously. I didn't at the time. That's why I later learned to play piano on my own. He was a gentle man who also loved to read. We had that in common. He would give me a book, ask me to read it and then we would discuss it on my next visit. He always made me feel special, that what I had to say mattered.

I love this photograph of Dad and Mom. He served in the Army during World War II. In his last letter before coming home, he told Mom that there was a song he had heard on the radio and he wanted her to sing it for him when he came home. He wanted her to figure out which song it was, so he wouldn't tell her the name of it. Not knowing if it was the same song, "You Belong to My Heart" was the first song she sang to him at his Welcome Home Party. Of course, it was the very song he had wanted her to sing, and it became their song.

She subsequently sang it to Dad, who was often embarrassed by the attention, at just about every family function.

That's me (see top right circle) in my second grade class. My all-time favorite teacher, Mrs. Florence Hobbs, is standing in the back (see top left circle). I kept in touch with her until she passed well into her 90's. What a lovely woman she was. She was a big influence on my life; she taught me to read and to love it, but, more importantly, she gave me a sense of self worth.

I used to visit her every summer on her birthday, June 20th. I would bake her a birthday cake and walk the mile and a half to her house to bring it to her. She was always so happy to see me. She moved to Cuba, in upstate New York, after getting married for the second time, at age sixty-nine, to her college sweetheart, Harold Saunders.

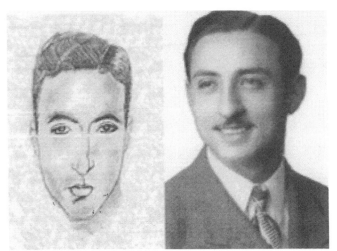

When I was about thirteen, I drew that sketch of Dad from a photo of him. Next to my sketch is one of my favorite photos of him. I loved his smile and wish he had used it more often. He loved to laugh, had a dry sense of humor, but was not a joyful person much of the time. But he was truly a "mush" in hiding. Few knew his true heart, but I was privileged to know it well.

He could make or fix just about anything. We would talk all the way to work and back summers and holidays when I filled in for the women in his office who wanted to be at home with their children. He was a very good man. He passed in 1995. I miss him so much.

****

This is just an idea of what you might want to do with your old family photographs. It was fun to do and will be something I can leave to my nephews and their families.

Acknowledgments

I would like to express my gratitude to the many people with whom I have rubbed shoulders in my life, for each was my teacher in some fundamental way. Some things cannot be taught, but they can be learned by observation or experience. I learned patience from some; kindness from others; perseverance from a few; and unconditional love from many.

I especially want to thank those who loved me through the writing of this book. To all those who provided support, talked things over with me, read my many drafts, made suggestions, offered comments, assisted in the editing, proofreading and design, thank you!

Comic-book artist Ghanshyam B with www.Comic-Book-Artists.com took my idea for the book cover and came up with a colorful and striking one, and also created the black and white character from which I created the internal illustrations.

I want to thank Oriah Mountain Dreamer for granting me permission to include a portion of her book, THE INVITATION © 1999. Published by HarperONE. All rights reserved. Presented with permission of the author. (www.oriah.org)

*I would like to thank my sister Rosemary for her humor, her constant love and support, and especially for her assurance that I would, indeed, become a successfully published author; after all, I **had** to, she said, so I could support her in her old age. (...just to set the record straight, **I** am the older sister.)*

I want to thank Maria, my beautiful niece-in-law, for giving me pats on the back and gentle kicks in the butt when I needed it to keep me on track. I want to thank my nephew John Sanzone for having the good sense to marry Maria, for his constant to-the-moon-and-back love, and for his invaluable technical help, remotely logging in when my computer needed a good spanking, and for working with me tirelessly on formatting and reformatting the book for publication.

I want to thank my parents John and Josephine, both gone now, for loving me and being proud of me. Growing up, I'm sure I sometimes thought they might have loved me better, but I always knew they could not have loved me more. Taking it all, mixing it up and shaking it together, they created exactly the kind of environment in which I needed to grow to become the person I am today. I love and miss them both very much.

I want to thank my beloved brother Johnny, also gone, for telling me he admired me for living an authentic life. He was a good, sweet man. I want to thank my sister-in-law Judy for loving my brother, and for having faith in me and my talent as a writer.

*I want to thank everyone in my big Sicilian family for the Sunday dinners with delicious food and abundant music. I especially want to thank my Uncle Joe, who inspired all of us to sing or play an instrument. He played a mean banjo – no, he played a **happy** banjo, leaning into the music like nobody else I've ever known or seen.*

*I thank all my friends for loving me, for laughing at, and sometimes being inspired by, my stories. I especially want to thank Valerie, Liz (Lisabeth), Millie, Maxine, Mindy and Shirley/Gypsi. Dr. Valerie Pellegrini, my friend and favorite philosopher, has shown me the finer virtues of friendship and Plato. She **gets** me. Lisabeth Reynolds, the author of <u>Purple Bowtie</u>, and a professional clown, is a good and supportive friend, who lovingly edited my first draft. Just being in her company and talking about our mutual writing projects, has always made me feel like a real writer. Millie Vega has always been a staunch believer in my spirituality and writing talent. I am grateful to have been her friend and, according to her, her spiritual teacher for over forty years. Maxine LeMarr, my talented and generous friend, who has performed at almost as many benefits as Bob Hope, has always made **me** feel special, and **that** is a priceless gift. Mindy McGee Alicea, musician and mensch, fellow member of the mutual admiration society, has always cheered me with her songs, and comforted me with her mensch-ness. Shirley Peters (AKA Gypsi O'Brion), a long-time friend who first introduced me to the world of radio and gently pushed me into doing standup comedy, has helped me learn many valuable lessons along the way.*

*And last, but surely not least, I want to thank my life partner, Barbara J. Lewis, whom I have loved for almost twenty wonderful years. She is my best audience, my one-woman cheering section. She is my rock and my heart. She has supported me emotionally, spiritually and financially those times between regular day jobs while I worked on this and other books. Without her love, her kindness, her encouragement, her faith **in** me and her praise **of** me, this book might never have been published. She has always provided the impetus to keep me going whenever I doubted myself.   Barbara, I am so grateful that we stumbled into this paradise together.*

159

Bibliography

I suppose every book I have ever read could be considered a source and, therefore, be included in this bibliography, but then we would need another book to list them all. So, what I have done is to list under "Bibliography" those books I have cited within this book, and to list a few more under "Suggested Reading."

Bach, Richard. Illusions: The Adventures of a Reluctant Messiah: Dell Publishing Co., Inc. 1977

Cameron, Julia. The Artist's Way: Tarcher 1992

Coudert, Jo. Advice from a Failure; Stein & Day, 1965

Cousins, Norman. Anatomy of an Illness: W.W. Norton & Co. 1979

Fox, Emmet. Power Through Constructive Thinking: Harper/SanFrancisco 1989 (Paperback) – Contains pamphlets "7-Day Mental Diet" and "Your Heart's Desire"

Freedman, Hy. Sex Link: The Three Billion Year Old Urge & What Animals Do About It: J. P. Lippincott Co. 1977

Fulcrum, Robert. Everything I ever need to know I learned in Kindergarten: A Balentine Book; A Random House Publication - 1988

Leedy, Jack J. (edited by) Poetry Therapy: J. B. Lippincott & Co. 1969

Leokum, Arkady. The Big Book of Tell Me Why: Barnes & Noble, 2000

Linamen, Karen S. I'm Not Suffering from Insanity; I'm Enjoying Every Minute of It!: Revell - 2002

Midler, Bette. The Saga of Baby Divine: Crown Publishers, 1983

Oriah Mountain Dreamer. <u>The Invitation:</u> Published by HarperONE, 1999

Polster, Erving. <u>Every Person's Life Is Worth A Novel</u>: W.W. Norton & Co.1987

Ruiz, Don Miguel. <u>The Four Agreements</u>: Amber-Allen Publishing, 1997

Thomas, Marlo. <u>The Right Words at the Right Time</u>: Pocket Books, 2002

Wagner, Jane. <u>The Search for Signs of Intelligence Life in the Universe (Book of the   script)</u>: First Perennial Library Edition, 1987

Walsh, Neal Donald. <u>Conversations with God: An Uncommon Dialogue</u>: Hampton Roads   Publishing Co., Inc. 1997

Zander, Benjamin and Roz. <u>The Art of Possibility</u>: Penguin Books, 2000

Suggested Reading

Baum, L. Frank. <u>The Wonderful Wizard of OZ</u>: George M. Hill Company 1900

Bristol, Claude. <u>The Magic of Believing</u>: Prentice-Hall, 1951

Brussat, Frederic and Mary Ann. <u>Spiritual Literacy: Reading the Sacred in Everyday Life</u>: Scribner 1996

Campbell, Joseph. <u>The Path of the Everday Hero</u>
<u>The Power of Myth (with Bill Moyers)</u>. Apostrophes Productions, Inc. 1988

Gerzon, Robert. <u>Finding Serenity in the Age of Anxiety</u>: MacMillan 1997

Moore, Thomas. <u>The Re-Enchantment of Everyday Life</u>: Harper Collins Pub. 1996

Myss, Caroline. <u>Sacred Contracts: Awakening Your Divine Potential</u>: Harmony Books 2001

Schucman, Helen. <u>A Course in Miracles</u>: Foundation for Inner Peace 1975

Villoldo, Alberto, Ph.D. <u>The Four Insights: Wisdom, Power, and Grace of the Earthkeepers</u>: Hay House, Inc. 2006

Made in the USA
Charleston, SC
13 June 2014